Making a Dozen Alike

A SEASONAL INDUSTRY

A STUDY OF THE MILLINERY TRADE IN NEW YORK

BY

MARY VAN KLEECK
DIRECTOR DIVISION OF INDUSTRIAL STUDIES
RUSSELL SAGE FOUNDATION

NEW YORK
RUSSELL SAGE FOUNDATION
MCMXVII

WM · F. FELL CO · PRINTERS
PHILADELPHIA

TABLE OF CONTENTS

LIST OF ILLUSTRATIONS

Photographs by Lewis W. Hine

LIST OF TABLES

TABLE PAGE

LIST OF TABLES

LIST OF TABLES

LIST OF TABLES

INTRODUCTION

SCOPE AND METHOD OF INVESTIGATION

UNIQUE opportunities were offered in two separate inquiries to secure the data presented in this volume. While the periods somewhat overlapped and many of the shops and a number of the workers appeared in both inquiries, the distinct angle of approach of each and the coordination of methods enabled us to check up the facts gained on wages, seasons, and conditions in the trade. Such a checking of data tends to minimize the ever-present dangers of inaccuracy which are all the more real in an investigation of a disorganized, fluctuating, and seasonal occupation like millinery. Even the layman with scant knowledge of the mysteries of the craft would agree that to attempt to classify and tabulate facts related to women's hats and to dignify the process by the name of industrial research is a bold undertaking. It is the more important, therefore, to describe somewhat in detail the character and methods of our studies and to give clearly the reasons for our confidence in the results, presented not as a contribution to the literature of fashion, but as a sober study of conditions more or less common to all industries characterized by seasonal fluctuations in employment.

The most important of these two inquiries was that conducted in co-operation with the Factory Investigating Commission of New York. Organized first in 1911 to study safety and sanitation in factories with a view to preventing the recurrence of such terrible disasters as the Triangle fire, which resulted in the deaths of 147 girls and women, the commission was authorized by the legislature of 1913 to make a study of wages in the state, and, if deemed necessary, to recommend some method of insuring adequate earnings for the workers who are now receiving less than the minimum sum necessary for healthful living. Evidently to the minds of the legislators and the constituents whom they represented, low pay was a menace to health and safety, quite as real as the danger from fire, and quite as logically an object of the attention of the commission. Obviously, it was impossible for the state's investigators to study all occupations. They selected four as likely to reveal the need for action—candy making, paper box making, the manufacture of men's shirts, and employment in department stores. As the Russell Sage Foundation had already begun an investigation of the millinery trade on its own behalf, but had not had access to any payrolls, it was agreed that the staff of the Committee on Women's Work acting with the commission and without expense to the state, should undertake to secure these wage data from millinery shops, following the same methods and using the same record forms as had been adopted in the other studies then being made by the commission. The examination of these payrolls was conducted during January and February of 1914, and the results were embodied in a report published by the commission in the autumn of 1914.* It was then arranged that the material could be used by the Russell Sage Foundation as part of its larger study of the millinery industry.

This larger study had been begun as early as 1908, when the Committee on Women's Work, then a department of the Alliance Employment Bureau, was conducting investigations financed by the Russell Sage Foundation but not yet part of the activities of the Foundation. The Alliance Employment Bureau was a philanthropic agency which found positions for girls and boys in factories and offices. At one time the bureau had charge of placing all graduates of the Manhattan Trade School for Girls, and it was at the request of the school that a preliminary study of the millinery trade was undertaken by the bureau's investigators.†

The purpose of this preliminary study was practical and immediate, to find out for the school how

* Wages in the Millinery Trade. New York State Factory Investigating Commission, 1914. Incorporated also as Part VII of Appendix IV of the Fourth Report of the New York State Factory Investigating Commission, 1915.

† These later became the investigators for the Committee on Women's Work. They were Miss Alice P. Barrows, who was in direct charge of this investigation under the supervision of the present writer, and Miss Louise C. Odencrantz, who took an active part in the field work as well as handling the compilation of statistics.

the graduates of its millinery classes fared in trade, and, in particular, whether seasonal conditions made the earning of a livelihood so precarious that the majority of the girls applying at the school should be discouraged from aspiring to be milliners. Such a question required very careful inquiry into trade conditions, not only including seasons, but wages, hours, processes of work, opportunities for learners, and chances for advancement; and information was sought not only from the girls already trained in the Manhattan Trade School, but from the graduates of other trade or technical schools,* from milliners who had learned in a shop and not in a class, and from employers who had or had not employed trade school girls.

Reports were made to the school from time to time on the basis of which changes were inaugurated, especially the adoption of the policy of giving applicants for training in millinery a full account of the conditions which they would encounter, and advising those who must be prepared as speedily as possible to earn a living to choose another occupation.†

* These included the Clara de Hirsch Home, Pratt Institute, the Hebrew Technical School for Girls, the McDowell School, the millinery classes of the public evening and summer schools, of the Young Women's Christian Association, of the Educational Alliance, and of Warren Goddard House, the Paris and Elite millinery schools, and several private classes.

† Later, a class in lampshade making was organized for girls in the millinery course in the hope that it might prove a feasible means of earning money in slack season. Aside from this practical use of the information by the school in its plan of training and by the bureau in

During that early period we realized that a thorough study of so variable and irregular a trade would require a larger amount of field work than we had yet accomplished, and especially some authoritative data from payrolls. The interviews with the workers and employers were continued in 1911 and 1912, concurrently with investigations of other trades, and in 1914, as has been already explained, the opportunity to study payrolls was secured through the Factory Investigating Commission.* In planning this payroll study we recognized that, because of the seasonal character of the trade, the facts needed in a legislative inquiry concerning the income of the workers were not the rates of wages in a selected week but the earnings week by week throughout the year, and the changes in the size of the force and the total payroll from season to season. We proposed, therefore, to make an intensive study of a few typical shops rather than a cursory inquiry into a larger number.

In a trade in which conditions and standards vary as widely as they do in millinery it was important to select a group of shops which should contain in miniature, as it were, all the diversity of type found in the trade itself. As the chemist can

its placement work, the results of the preliminary inquiry were published in two comparatively brief articles:—

Barrows, Alice P., and Van Kleeck, Mary: How Girls Learn the Millinery Trade. *The Survey*, XXIV: 105–113 (April 16, 1910).

Barrows, Alice P.: The Training of Millinery Workers. Proceedings of Academy of Political Science (October, 1910).

* In tabulating the final statistics no records secured prior to October, 1911, were used.

determine the composition of the whole body of water in a reservoir by analyzing a small sample, so the investigator of industry may legitimately portray all the essential facts in a trade by intensive study of a small group, provided the group be wisely selected. In this investigation, as will be shown later, we were able to cover a large enough proportion of the trade to justify confidence in the results. Both chance and discretion were factors in our selection. We first made a card catalogue of the millinery shops in Manhattan* listed in the industrial directory of the New York State Department of Labor, arranged the cards by streets and numbers, and drew out every fifth card. The names and addresses of these were then compared with the records of our previous investigation and, by a process of selection and substitution, a list of about 75 establishments was finally prepared. Our investigators soon discovered that the small neighborhood shops of the Third Avenue type must be eliminated because no payroll records were kept in them. This very practical difficulty resulted, of course, in limiting our study to those establishments which are large enough and sufficiently well organized to keep wage records, so that in the end our list was reduced to 57.†

The group which we investigated included large and fashionable establishments on Fifth Avenue,

* For the reasons for selecting the borough of Manhattan instead of the entire city, see discussion of the trade on pp. 54–55.

† For the number of records secured from these, see Table 1, p. 10.

aspiring shops on the side streets as close as possible to the highway of fashionable trade but not yet fully "arrived," less ambitious firms on streets and avenues farther removed from the leaders of the industry, small shops on Third Avenue, big supply houses on lower Broadway, and the wholesale establishments which have moved uptown (portending a general northward move for wholesale millinery as for other industries on Manhattan Island); the more humble wholesale factory on Division Street, which ships its cheap products to Texas and other distant states, and on the same block the typical Division Street retail shop with its unique method of soliciting custom by stationing on the sidewalk a "puller-in," a stalwart woman who seizes passersby and drags them into the store, there to be dealt with by an equally importunate saleswoman.

In reality, we have three distinct methods of classifying millinery shops: first, as to method of selling, that is, as wholesale or retail; second, as to location, with differences so marked in different sections of the city as to make the name of the street, Fifth Avenue, Third Avenue, Grand Street, Division Street, or Broadway, a descriptive adjective conveying to any one familiar with these localities a distinct impression of the kind of millinery to be found there; and third, as to grade of hat made, with dozens all alike of the so-called ready-to-wear headgear at one end of the scale, and at the other the unique and distinctive creation of the expert designer. One employer, speaking somewhat scornfully of the lack of originality displayed by most milliners, named as "the creators in the business" only five firms, his own among them. We were encouraged to note that we had secured payroll statistics from all of them and presumably, therefore, we knew the trade at its best.

RECORD CARDS USED

To secure the facts necessary for a study of seasonal fluctuations in employment in a trade and the effect of these on the regularity of work of the employes requires several sets of records. The yearly history of each millinery establishment as it was revealed on the payroll was copied for the calendar year 1913 on schedules. The first, designated as Card A,* showed the total number of women† employes in the millinery workroom and the total wages paid to them each week in 1913. The second, Card B, was filled for each worker whose name appeared on the payroll at any time during the year, and showed her total earnings from that establishment in twelve months. The information to be derived from these two sets of facts is, of course, of the utmost importance in an analysis of irregularity of employment. Weekly changes in the size of the force show variations in the demand for workers. These do not indicate,

* An illustrative set of records will be found in Appendix A, p. 237.

† For the reasons for limiting the study to women workers, see discussion of trade, pp. 13, 41 ff. and 54.

A "Puller-in" at Work

A "Puller-in" for a Division Street Shop

however, whether the workers were employed full time, part time, or overtime. The best index of the amount of labor utilized is the number of dollars paid in wages, and the plotting of this curve on a scale co-ordinate with that of numbers at work gives a true picture of fluctuations in the labor force used by the industry. Weekly changes in the labor force, however, do not represent the full measure of irregularity of employment. Not only does the total force in an establishment vary in size but the personnel changes, and the job of any one worker may be longer or shorter than the period of greatest activity in the shops. It is the individual records which show the length of each worker's employment in one shop in the year, and the total number of individuals employed for any period in the course of the twelve months, a number much larger than the maximum force on any selected date.

To have limited the study to these facts, valuable as they are, would have been to miss much important information about the workers and, indeed, to have failed to discover the real significance in the wage data. We needed to know how long these milliners had been in their present positions, how long they had been in the trade, how old they were, whether they were native born or foreigners, married or single, boarding or living at home. Of course, only the group employed in the workroom at the date of the investigation was available for such inquiry. The method of securing the facts was to draw off certain data from the payroll for the week nearest the date of our visit to that establishment.* To Card C were thus transferred the wage rate, earnings, method of payment,—by the week or by the piece,—regular hours, and actual hours of work in the selected week for each employe. In order to correlate these facts with personal information not available on payrolls a separate card (D) was handed to each milliner at work in the shop, on which to record her age, nationality, length of experience, and living conditions.

Table 1 shows the number of shops investigated in the two main branches of the trade, the maximum force employed in these shops, and the number of records secured from workers (Card D), from current payrolls (Card C), and from yearly payrolls (Cards A and B).

We secured records from 57 shops, of which 29 sold hats at retail and 28 at wholesale.† The payrolls for the current week were copied in 56 of them, and thus information regarding rates of pay and actual earnings in one week was obtained for 1,951 workers. To match these schedules, cards were filled out by girls in the workroom to the number

* Obviously, the exact date varied for different shops. In the discussion which follows we refer to this record of the current payroll as distinct from the annual payroll, which covered in every case the year 1913.

† In the investigation of wages in department stores made by the Factory Investigating Commission, payroll statistics were secured for the millinery workrooms in 21 stores in New York City and 34 stores in eight other cities of New York state; namely, Buffalo, Rochester, Syracuse, Utica, Schenectady, Albany, Troy, and Kingston. This information is summarized in Appendix C, pp. 250 ff

TABLE I.—NUMBER OF SHOPS INCLUDED IN THE PAYROLL INVESTIGATION, MAXIMUM FORCE OF WOMEN EMPLOYED IN THE HAT TRIMMING DEPARTMENTS, AND NUMBER OF RECORDS SECURED, BY BRANCH OF THE TRADE

	Retail shops	Wholesale shops	All shops
Shops for which records were received	29	28	57[a]
Maximum force employed . . .	839	1,711	2,550
Shops supplying			
Workers' reports	29	25	54
Payroll for current week . .	29	27	56
Payroll for full year, 1913 . .	19	21	40
Records secured			
Workers' reports	470	893	1,363
Payroll for current week . . .	546	1,405	1,951
Payroll for full year, 1913 . .	1,143	2,840	3,983

[a] In all, 65 firms were visited, but of these two had failed and were out of business, one made only straw or felt hats, while two never employed more than one worker, and the remaining three did not keep permanent payrolls.

of 1,363, but for various reasons the reports from workers could not be secured for the remaining 588 of the 1,951 on the current payrolls. In some shops, for instance, the employers objected to their distribution, and because of this lack of co-operation on their part satisfactory returns could not be secured. In other cases, some of the girls whose names had appeared on the payroll had left since the last pay day, or were temporarily absent. Transcriptions of the payroll for the entire calendar year of 1913 were made in 40 shops, including one in which the payroll for the week of the investigation was not copied. In the other 17 shops for which some information was secured, the statistics for the whole year were not available, because these firms did not keep payrolls showing individual earnings or had not preserved them for the year, or, in a few cases, had changed hands or had been established within twelve months. In the 40 shops studied for the year the maximum force in the busy season was 2,550, but the total number of names appearing on the payrolls at any time in the course of the year was 3,983.

This last figure represents really the total number of jobs held in these shops rather than the total number of workers, for in some instances we found the same worker appearing on the payrolls of different establishments, showing change of employment from one shop to another; and undoubtedly other cases of the same kind would have been discovered had it been possible to match up the records with any degree of accuracy. Obviously, however, even the appearance of the same name on the records of two or more shops is not conclusive proof that it is the same worker, unless her name or her work record is unusual enough to warrant such an assumption. The fairest figure to use in estimating the proportion of the trade investigated is not the total number of names on the payrolls in a year, which is indicative rather of fluctuations in employment and changes in the force, but the combined maximum force in the busy season in the shops investigated; that is, 2,550. According to figures in the industrial directory of the New York State Department of

Labor, to be discussed later (pages 54–55), the number of women employed in Manhattan shops in 1912 was 7,933. These were the latest available figures at the time the investigation was planned. Thus the shops investigated by us represented 32 per cent of the women milliners employed in Manhattan, or 29 per cent of the 8,885 counted by the labor department throughout the city.* As will be indicated later, the millinery industry employs men, but almost wholly in manufacturing rather than trimming, so that the limitation of our inquiry to women workers was due to logic and not prejudice.

ATTITUDE OF EMPLOYERS

Our reception by employers, even though we came as sworn agents of the state with proper badges and credentials, was not always cordial. Sometimes we were met by a hostile bookkeeper, to whom his books are no doubt of consummate importance, containing secrets not to be lightly entrusted to the prying agents of the legislature. One of them assured us that the law authorizing such an inquiry was unjust and could not be enforced. He asked how the investigator

* If the census figures showing 13,000 women milliners in New York City in 1910 be used (see page 54), the proportion investigated was 20 per cent. This, however, is a less accurate figure than that of the Department of Labor, since the census counted all milliners whether working in shops or at home, whereas the industrial directory included only shops employing one or more workers. It was the shop which was the unit in our study.

would feel if he were to demand information about her domestic expenditures. Moreover, the inclusion of millinery in such a study was very unwise, since its conditions were unlike those of any other industry and the seasonal variations made any regularity of income impossible. As another employer expressed it, when we explained that we wanted to know the annual earnings of milliners, "There are no annual earnings in millinery. Don't you know it's a seasonal trade?"

Another employer, one of "the creators in the business," was courteous but reluctant to show his payroll, owing to "the confidential nature of the millinery trade," and the supposed eagerness of every other employer to know what this shop paid to its designers. A woman who declared that she, in her youth, worked much harder than the girls nowadays, objected to the investigation because it would make her employes feel too independent and would give them a notion that their wages should be higher. Anyway, she felt that there was ample remedy for low wages in the fact that if a girl "does not like her pay in one shop, she can go to another." Some of the other women who own shops, and an occasional man, increased our comfort in our difficult task of copying payrolls in whatever corner of office or workroom happened to be unoccupied, by such cordial remarks as, "It's an awful bother having you here. You're in our way. It is a shame for them (the lawmakers of the state) to bother people this way in the busy season."*

None of these employers blocked us in our inquiry, of course, although they sometimes made our task a difficult one. We note their attitude because it shows how great is the need for just such investigations to compel realization of the public concern in wages paid and the public's right to know the facts. Those employers, a minority we must confess, who made no objection whatever and who rather facilitated the investigation in every possible way, have earned our respect and appreciation.

FORM OF PAYROLLS

The real difficulty in this part of the inquiry, however, was not in converting employers but in getting the facts we wanted from the payrolls commonly used. Some description of their diverse forms is important both in interpreting wage statistics in this study and in discussing future wage investigations. In some shops visited no payroll was found, the stubs of check books or

* One of the partners in a wholesale firm said that he had no objection to furnishing the information, if only the state would ask for all that was needed at one time. A short time before, he said, he had filled out a blank for the department of labor, showing number employed, hours of work, and other facts similar to those for which we asked. In another wholesale shop the employer and his wife, who are partners in management,—a frequent occurrence in this trade,—could see no use in the investigation, especially as theirs was an industry different from any other business and, because of its seasonal variability, entitled to exemption from all legislative regulation. "It's worse than playing the stock market."

a stray memorandum showing merely the total weekly outlay for wages. But the absence of a record was not the only difficulty encountered. The payrolls* themselves were often obscure for our purposes, and the only item of information common to them all was the wage received. In some was recorded the full name, and in one instance the address was entered once each season. In others only the first name appeared. In establishments using a time clock, with a card stamped automatically when the worker punches the clock at the time of entry and when she leaves, it is usual to designate each worker on the payroll by her time clock number, although sometimes the name also appears. The actual time of work is then recorded and deductions are made for days lost and, often, for minutes of tardiness. This careful

* Of all that we examined, just one stands out in memory as a model of convenience for the investigator seeking facts for a continuous, individual record. This was a loose-leaf book with a separate sheet for each employe. On the first line was a space for the full name, the department in which she worked, and the dates of entering and leaving. The column headings gave the date of payment, rate, lost time, net earnings, charges, amount paid, and space for a weekly signature after the words "received the amount opposite my name." These columns were repeated twice on the same page, giving space for consecutive entries for many weeks. When a girl is laid off, her record is filed and can be continued if she returns. It is unnecessary for the bookkeeper to copy the names and rates of pay of the workers weekly, as is done in those shops using an ordinary blank book with a separate page for each week instead of a page for each employe. On the other hand, the weekly list is more convenient for securing totals. To avoid the necessity for copying names or numbers every week, some books had a stub arrangement so that the earnings for a number of weeks, sometimes four, sometimes thirteen, could be entered in columns opposite a single list. One large firm had a loose-leaf book with a page for a week's earnings which matched a list, renewed twice a year.

checking of time applies, however, only to the so-called week workers, those who receive a definite amount per week. No such entry of hours is made for those whose earnings are calculated on the piece-work basis, whereby a definite rate is paid according to the number of hats trimmed, and time does not enter into the calculation. Piece workers are often designated by number only.

The use of numbers instead of names makes the tracing of a worker through a record of several weeks exceedingly difficult, for the reason that numbers are reassigned repeatedly in the course of a year. Marked differences in earnings, the statement of the bookkeeper, or long lapses of time between entries were the chief checks on accuracy of identification in those shops in which the names did not appear on the payrolls. The same checks were necessary when only the first names were used. One could not be sure always that Annie, in the autumn, was the same Annie as in the spring.

The lack of a time record for piece workers made it impossible also to determine whether the earnings represented a full week's work, or overtime, or two days of employment. Home work also was an unrecorded factor sometimes in apparently high earnings, since in some shops the girls take work home at night and the family may help. Their combined efforts will appear in the total week's output for one worker. Another serious difficulty was the entry of a single payment for a team of two or three workers. This was encountered only among piece workers, never among week workers, and then in only one or two shops; and it was obviated by searching inquiry on the part of the investigators, but the possibility of error was not thereby entirely eliminated.

Numerous other annoyances and difficulties beset us in the endeavor to secure accurate data from the payrolls. Sometimes part payments were made in hats or millinery trimmings. Sometimes a worker drew out her wages in advance, and was paid from the cash box with an entry in the daily cash account but none in the payroll. In one shop the dressmaking department worked nine hours a day, fifty-four a week, and the milliners eight and one-half hours a day and fifty-one a week. For the sake of uniformity, the nine-hour standard was used throughout the payroll, and for our purposes it was necessary to translate the figures for hours worked into the milliner's eight and one-half hour day.* In a wholesale factory, until a few weeks before the investigation, the method of entering piece workers' earnings had been to record totals only, and to study individuals it was necessary to go back to the individual slips made out in the workroom to show piece workers' output. These were resurrected in dusty

* An entry of eight and three-quarters hours meant that a milliner had been late fifteen minutes, and that her actual day's work was eight and one-quarter hours long. A twenty-two and one-half hour week was obviously two and a half days on the fifty-four hour basis, or twenty-one and one-quarter hours in a fifty-one hour week.

piles from the vaults. Perhaps the climax of our difficulties came in the discovery of two instances in which the payroll was in cipher. CAE indicated $6.00, and KTA, $2.50. In one of these shops the rate only was shown on the payroll with the amounts deducted for any cause, such as tardiness, and the actual earnings did not appear.

As social legislation advances, and commissions are appointed to secure information about industrial establishments, the absence of uniformity and the lack of accuracy in keeping payrolls become a serious matter. Legislation, prescribing some method of recording this information, is urgently needed but should be framed only after full consideration of the many uses to which it may be put.*

PERSONAL INTERVIEWS

The statistics secured from payrolls and from cards filled out by employes were reinforced by interviews with employers as to methods of hiring workers and determining wages, processes of work and organization of the force, plans for training learners, hours of labor, and overtime. Some of the workers were also interviewed at home to learn more about their trade careers, the conditions encountered by them, and especially the time lost from work because of slack seasons. These inter-

* For instance, we were told that the form which we found most convenient, a page for each worker, had been proved unmanageable by agents who needed to know the total payroll in connection with insurance for workmen's compensation.

views were in accordance with the plan of the investigation which antedated our work for the Factory Investigating Commission.

The number of women interviewed at home in the entire investigation was 252. The number of employers interviewed was 149, representing shops employing a maximum force of 3,781 women. These included the establishments from which payroll data were obtained. The names of the girls to be interviewed were secured from a variety of sources, as Table 2 shows.

TABLE 2.—SOURCES OF NAMES OF WOMEN MILLINERS INTERVIEWED AT HOME, OCTOBER, 1911, TO AUGUST, 1914

Source of name	Names secured from each specified source
New York State Factory Investigating Commission (millinery payroll study)	123
Public evening schools	64
Relative or friend of worker	31
Trade school	11
Milliners' union	10
Settlement	5
Girls' Friendly Society	4
Alliance Employment Bureau	3
Women's Trade Union League	1
Total	252

It will thus be seen that nearly half of the names came from the payrolls of millinery shops examined in 1914. About one-fourth, 64, were girls attending classes in New York public evening schools, whose names had been secured through another investigation.* Relatives or friends, many of them milliners, gave us the names of 31, trade schools 11, the secretary of the milliners' union 10, and other organizations 13. An introduction from a friend or a teacher would enable the investigator to gain the confidence of the girl at once and to enlist her interest in our purposes. To secure the co-operation of those who became known to us through our payroll study, we asked them to help us to decide what the minimum wage for milliners ought to be and whether any legislation was needed to secure it, and the majority showed a lively interest in our questions.

We used four cards† to record the facts gained in these interviews. The first (E) provided for facts about the worker's schooling, family conditions, nativity, yearly earnings, and expenditures; the second (F), for a record of all her positions; the third (G), for her report of the millinery shop in which she had been most recently employed, and the fourth (H), for the investigator's record of a shop. The first choice of establishments to be investigated previous to the payroll study was determined by the girls' records. All their present places of employment in millinery were selected. This list was then lengthened by the addition of certain well-known establishments or by shops in certain districts about which we desired more in-

* The results of this study of girls attending evening classes are published in Working Girls in Evening Schools. Russell Sage Foundation Publication. New York, Survey Associates, 1914.

† These are reproduced in Appendix A, pp. 244–247.

formation. Their types and the number in different neighborhoods will be discussed in a later chapter.

Among employers the topic of trade school training proved especially interesting, and made it possible for us to secure information from them even before we were armed with state authority. The long history of the inquiry revealed in the detailed account in these pages is further evidence of the reliability of the data submitted, since our continued months of observation and investigation gave us, as we have already stated, an exceptional opportunity to check up results and to test conclusions.

For instance, in one wholesale shop we interviewed the employer first in 1908, again in 1911, and copied the payroll in 1914. We also had the reports of 15 girls employed there from time to time. This is not a unique case, although it is, of course, not typical of the majority of shops. One of the workers interviewed in 1909 was found employed in a shop in which the payroll was studied in 1914. Another, also investigated in 1909, had found work in a Fifth Avenue shop immediately after our interview with her and her name was found on the payroll there five years later. All the facts which she gave as to birthplace, years in the trade, and age at beginning work were found to tally exactly with our previous record of her. This experience in finding in 1914 workers already known to us was repeated in several instances.

According to a forewoman of many years' experience in millinery, to whom the manuscript of this book was submitted, conditions in the trade in 1916–17, both as to wages and as to seasons, showed marked improvement over conditions in 1914, when the field work of the investigation was completed. Whether this was due to the industrial prosperity throughout the country or to a more fundamental and lasting change in the industry itself, could not be finally determined. In any event, the facts showing the effects of irregular employment in an occupation like millinery must remain significant so long as seasonal fluctuations continue to cause unemployment in any trade.

The investigators who took part in various stages of the inquiry were Miss Alice P. Barrows, Miss Louise C. Odencrantz, Miss Marie H. Hourwich, whose knowledge of Jewish, Russian, Polish, and German was useful in interviewing foreign-born milliners, Miss Elizabeth L. Meigs, Dr. Anna M. Richardson, and the writer. Miss Odencrantz and Miss Henriette R. Walter are responsible for the statistics.

As one reads the remarks of worker after worker and employer after employer as they are reported on the card records, one is impressed most of all, perhaps, by numerous contradictions and conflicts of opinion. "The best workers have the longest seasons," said one employer. "The best workers are laid off early. They are too expensive to keep," declared another. "It is better for a girl to learn the trade in a wholesale shop where she must make the whole hat. In retail she may work steadily at bandeaux," was one girl's opinion. "There is very little real millinery in most wholesale places," was the opinion of another, "it's just putting together materials already prepared by machine."

We are reminded of the preface of an eighteenth century book entitled A General Description of All Trades. Here the author appeals to "the candid reader" in words which any investigator will echo from the heart. "Consider," he writes, "how many different persons must have been consulted to gain so much intelligence as is herein communicated; and add to this the oddness and variety of men's tempers, on being asked three or four civil questions, the answering which was no trouble, nor could be any detriment; yet some were shy, others jealous; some testy; others sour; nay, some quite angry, thinking one was come as a spy to steal the secrets of their trade; and besides all this, several of the same trade or business were met with who gave very different accounts."

The author, however, overlooked the fact that several conflicting statements may all be true. To draw out the truth from them all is the task of the investigator. It is a talent demanded pre-eminently in describing the millinery trade.

CHAPTER I

THE SIGNIFICANCE OF THE TRADE

THEY will tell you in the millinery shops of New York that no employer can control the length of the seasons. Fashion, women, and the weather are alone responsible. Everybody in the business must accept its whimsical irregularities as part of the established order, and only theorists or reformers would dream of suggesting the possibility of control of a situation created by admittedly uncontrollable conditions. To be sure, a general impression prevails that the lot of the milliner grows worse instead of better, that seasons are shorter and styles more fickle than in former days, but no employer takes the trouble to analyze why this should be so, or to reason that if changes are in progress it is conceivable that intelligent direction might turn them to the advantage of the industry. The old laissez-faire theory is on trial again in the millinery shops of New York as it is in many another modern industry.

Meanwhile, economists and reformers have abandoned the doctrine that drifting is an inevitable procedure characteristic of the economic world, and have formulated new ideas of social control. In such times of stress as prevailed after the beginning of the war in 1914, they were roused to action as never before by the spectacle of hundreds of thousands of men and women out of work, deprived of a chance to earn a livelihood. Whether the cause be the setting loose of new and terrible forces of hatred between nations, the turning of plowshares into bullets, and the building of battleships instead of the construction of railroads, or whether it be an unexplained and unexpected check in business enterprise, or a recurrent falling off in demand for labor, unemployment is recognized by all who know anything about the lives of the workers as a disaster productive of great personal suffering and of widespread social evils. To the social reformer today,—and by social reformer we mean every man and woman who has a vision of what the social order ought to be and who believes that it can be made like the vision,—to recognize an evil is to set about changing it. Nothing socially disastrous is inevitable. Such faith, however, if it is to be fulfilled, must be particularized. It must apply wherever the conditions of modern industry press heavily upon the workers,—in an artificial flower factory and in the mammoth steel works, in subway construction, and in the making of a woman's hat.

This, then, is the first and the fundamental reason for analyzing the facts about the millinery trade. It is to a marked degree a seasonal occupation. Study of it should illuminate the whole problem of unemployment and irregular work. It challenges the reformer to particularize his faith that either seasonal fluctuations can be eliminated or their social evils diminished to the vanishing point. This faith is in conflict with the opinion of almost everybody in the trade that short seasons are inevitable.

The millinery industry is significant also for the light which it throws on the economic position of women, both as consumers and as workers. Doubtless the average man and many sober-minded women would list women's hats among the luxuries of the world, a luxury, too, which reflects the mind of woman. Wearing hats is not a universal necessity. In some countries scarfs or veils prove quite as effective as covering for the head. Few would have the courage to claim that the amazing headgear of the eighteenth century, when women's heads were surmounted by miniature battleships, steeples, or temples to Cupid, could be regarded as an economic necessity. In France, extravagance in trimming became so unbridled that Richelieu forbade the purchase of "Milanese" goods.* A distinction must be made, however, between the necessity for covering the head as a protection against heat or cold, and the luxury of ornamentation. In this country, certainly, climate and

* Webb, Sydney (Editor): Seasonal Trades. Chapter on Millinery by Charlotte K. Saunders, p. 211. London, Constable and Co., 1912.

social custom together have made hats for women or men as necessary a part of the standard of living as shoes, stockings, or gloves. The line is more or less distinct, however, between the kind of article needed for proper clothing and the choice of such materials or ornaments as may make the greater part of its value a real luxury. It is above this line that fashion exerts its influence as a highly significant expression of the social mind with far-reaching effects on conditions of employment.

The millinery trade, however, has become an integral part of the business of clothing the world and his wife, with a legitimate claim as such to recognition as a fundamental industry supplying one of the necessary elements in a proper standard of living. On the other hand, millinery is also one of the products of the world's work, reflecting the foolish extravagance which is the main factor in creating extreme fickleness in market demands. Although extravagance is not limited to one sex, it would not be difficult for a student of feminism to trace a connection between expensive fashions in millinery and the characteristics and position of the present-day woman of leisure.

Tempting as such a subject would be, nevertheless, it is millinery as an occupation for working women, rather than hats as an indication of feminine psychology and a measure of social advancement, which is the subject of our investigation. It gives employment to 13,000 women in New

York City,* 13,700 in London,† 19,400 in Paris,‡ 4,400 in Berlin,§ 5,800 in Chicago,|| 3,800 in Philadelphia,** and it is found as a wage-earning pursuit in many a smaller community where at least one woman earns her living by making other women's hats. As one owner of a small shop expressed it: "Millinery is a safe trade to learn because a good milliner can find work anywhere on the globe. The same design may not suit everybody, but the foundation work is the same the world over." It is not a highly centralized, localized industry, and, in a sense, a milliner may carry her occupation with her instead of being tied by it to one locality. Moreover, it does not require a large plant. One worker, acting both as employer and employe, may conduct a business in her own parlor. Finally, in learning the trade a woman may become her own milliner even if she does not make use of the talent as a wage-earning pursuit.

As this description implies, millinery affords an interesting illustration of diverse forms of industrial organization within the same field of work.

* See page 54.

† Census of England and Wales, 1911. Vol. X, Occupations and Industries. Pt. I, p. 37.

‡ Ministère du Travail et de la Prévoyance Sociale. Résultats Statistique du Recénsement Général de la Population, effectué le 4 Mars, 1906. Tome II, p. 23.

§ Statistiches Jahrbuch der Stadt Berlin, 1908–11, p. 358.

|| Thirteenth United States Census, 1910. Population, Vol. IV, Occupation Statistics, p. 546.

** Ibid., p. 590.

It affords interesting contrasts with other industries which, nevertheless, have in common with it the same problem of irregular employment due to seasonal demands. Paper box making, for instance, is distinctly a factory industry and machinery is essential. The processes vary, of course, with different kinds and sizes of boxes. Part of the hand work is sometimes done in tenement homes, but always the factory is in control. We do not find women setting up box-making shops in their own parlors. Nor do we find any degree of competition between the machine-made products and such articles as hand-made jewel cases or cretonne-covered novelties. Logically all of these are boxes, but actually they form separate industries having little or no reaction on each other. In millinery, on the other hand, the machine-sewed straw or the pressed velvet or felt may be in the ascendancy one season, to the joy of the wholesale dealer, who turns these hats out in quantities, while a few months later fashion will demand hand-sewn hats of more varied design to suit personal taste, and the retailer will be extraordinarily busy. The reaction of one branch of the trade on the other is constant. The machine is not having an easy victory over the handicraft. A shop may employ one worker or three hundred. Millinery will be the product of a highly organized factory on one block and the occupation of the home on the next. Social control over the mighty steel works owned by a single large corporation would seem to be more easily gained than the regulation of the many diverse types of organization represented in the millinery industry.

It is doubtless because millinery is still largely a hand occupation, and because it has inherent attractions in offering scope for taste in line and color, that it has been one of the first trades chosen for experiments in industrial education. In New York City it is taught in public trade and technical schools, and in so-called prevocational classes, and it is offered as a course in the public evening schools. Whether these classes accomplish desired results in developing efficient milliners, whether they tend to increase unduly the supply of workers in an occupation which many believe to be already overcrowded, whether the standards of employment as they affect the workers are high enough to justify the expenditure of public funds in providing this form of apprenticeship; whether, indeed, conditions of employment, especially wages and seasons, deserve consideration in a program of public industrial training,—all these are questions which make the facts about millinery important to the educators.

Present standards of labor legislation, also, are illustrated especially in the large establishments which partake of the nature of factories. Indeed, it was the employment of a milliner more than fifty-four hours a week in Ohio which resulted in a recent decision of the United States Supreme Court affirming the constitutionality of limiting by law the weekly hours of women's work in factories.* In New York, as in Ohio, millinery shops are factories, and the labor laws of the state apply to them in all particulars, including the prohibition of child labor, the requirements as to sanitation and safety, and the regulation of hours of work of women. Indeed, it may be said, that the possibility of more adequate control of such conditions as are revealed in the millinery trade through the extension of labor legislation, possibly in provisions for determining wage standards, is the large question which inspired this investigation.

* Case of Hawley *vs.* Walker (Ohio). 232 U. S. 217. Decision handed down Feb. 24, 1914.

CHAPTER II

FACTS ABOUT THE TRADE

THE man who needs a new hat in New York purchases it ready-made from a retail hat dealer, from a clothing shop or a department store, or possibly he may place an order specifying size, color, shape, material, or the position of the bow. He has no other choice. To the woman, the possibilities are more varied and distracting, not only in style of trimming but in method of purchase. If she be an expert in home arts she may be her own milliner. She may buy the shape and the decoration and combine the two. The shape may be a wire or buckram frame to be covered with hand-sewn straw, silk, or velvet. Or it may be machine-made and pressed, ready for the trimming and the lining. If she cannot make or trim her own hat a friend in the block who, perchance, works in a millinery shop by day, may trim it for her. If she be so thrifty as to be unwilling to pay for such service, she may purchase her supplies in the shop of a millinery dealer who advertises that hats bought in the shop will be trimmed free of charge, or she may seek out a department store in which she may select a shape at one counter and carry it to another where a saleswoman makes bows of ribbon and places them in the proper position while the customer waits. If such manœuvering be inconvenient, one of the many varieties of retail shops may come to the rescue; either one which sells ready-to-wear hats purchased from a wholesale house, or one which displays stock made in its own workrooms, or one which takes orders from individual customers. These various methods of purchasing suggest the divisions of the trade. An understanding of them is necessary before the tasks of the girls employed in the workrooms can be visualized or the characteristic trade problems analyzed.

The first broad division, already described, is based on the method of selling designated by the terms wholesale and retail, common to many other occupations. Under the heading of retail would be classed all milliners who deal directly with the wearers of the hats, whether they be "parlor milliners" without employes, modest managers of small neighborhood shops, or the owners of large and fashionable establishments. The wholesalers are those from whom the sellers of hats, the retail shop owners, the jobbers, or the department stores make their purchases. Many of the larger retail shops have also a wholesale trade, selling models to wholesale or retail dealers. Within these two main divisions is a great variety in the grade of the product, in the market supplied, and consequently in the type of workmanship and the general organization of the shop. Table 3 shows the loca-

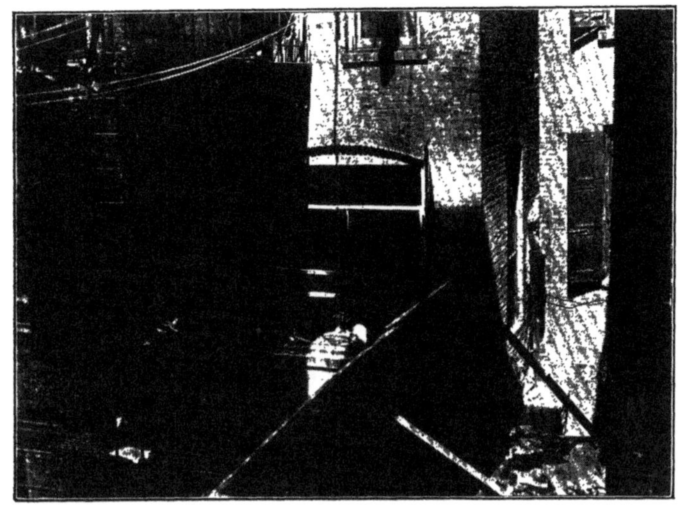

Rear Windows of a Workroom on Division Street

Millinery on Division Street

tion of all the shops investigated by us, and because a certain kind of trade tends to become characteristic of a certain neighborhood, it indicates more or less accurately the variety in types of work.

TABLE 3.—LOCATION OF MILLINERY ESTABLISHMENTS INVESTIGATED, BY BRANCH OF THE TRADE

Branch of trade and location	Establishments investigated in each specified location
RETAIL	
Neighborhood shops:	
Lower East Side	13
Lower West Side	2
Upper East Side	16
Upper West Side	24
Total neighborhood shops	55
Fifth Avenue section	41
Sixth Avenue section	3
Wall Street section	2
Total retail establishments	101
WHOLESALE	
Lower Broadway section	33
Uptown loft section	7
Division Street section	6
Total wholesale establishments	46
CONTRACTORS	2
Grand total	149

We may picture Fifth Avenue as the goal of all retail milliners. It is probable that with the traditional American spirit even the owner of the small shop on Avenue A or First Avenue is not without hope that some day she, too, may work in the blaze of light which is supposed to illumine the center of fashion. If one's location is nearer the leaders of the trade, on Lexington Avenue, Madison Avenue, or at a number less than one hundred east or west, one's ambition is correspondingly greater as its satisfaction seems more possible. In the actual history of several shops one may trace the movement upward in the scale of fashion. A milliner interviewed in 1912 had just moved from Seventh Avenue to Fifth Avenue, and was somewhat anxiously trying to adjust her methods to the demands of an entirely different class of customers. Another, starting on the middle East Side, with three or four girls employed, was finally running a prosperous business on Madison Avenue. Another was on Lexington Avenue in 1909, and in 1914 on Fifty-eighth Street, a few doors from Fifth Avenue.

These changes are the indications of individual success. They are not part of the general tendency to move which affects almost all trades in New York. For example, one of the largest and oldest of the retail firms had its beginnings seventy years ago not far from Chatham Square on the lower East Side, then moved to Canal Street, then to Twenty-third Street, and is finally established some thirty blocks farther north. More recently the wholesale shops have begun to move from lower Broadway as far north as the forties, whereas five years ago scarcely any wholesale millinery shops were to be found north of Fourteenth Street. The movement of the wholesale industry is, of course, determined by the convenience of buyers, many of whom come from out of town. Similarly, many of the largest retail establishments with a national reputation attract both wholesale buyers and customers from distant cities who come to New York on shopping expeditions.

The small retail shops, on the other hand, cater to the demands of a limited neighborhood. One "madame" on Columbus Avenue specializes in hats for domestic servants, and gives the members of that profession a 10 per cent reduction. Her clientele pleases her better than the charge accounts of their employers. "The servant girl trade is the best I have," she said. "They pay cash and they don't demand so much." A few enterprising milliners have opened shops in the financial district, following the movement of women in business. They do not expect customers from uptown, but aim rather to catch the trade of the business woman who has no time for distant shopping and will welcome a chance to make purchases near her office. An Eighth Avenue shop has the unusual record of twenty-five years at one address, building up a trade with working people who live nearby. "We buy ready-trimmed hats mostly," said the owner. "There is no need now for much trimming." On the other side of the city, in a First Avenue shop, we were told that "our trade is different here. It is not so particular as on 'the Avenue.' People buy a shape for 98 cents and a bit of trimming and have it sewed on. That is all there is to it. Sometimes we get $5.00 for a hat, but it is very unusual and people seldom leave an order." Another First Avenue milliner said that she always went downtown to the wholesalers for her ideas and that she bought her hats ready trimmed.

Many of the retail shops are, indeed, chiefly distributing centers for the wholesale trade. A Harlem employer, with a neighborhood trade large enough to keep 40 saleswomen busy in the season, said that he employed only eight milliners and yet that his was the largest workroom in that district of the city. He maintained his workroom only for alterations and for a very few custom orders. He also sold millinery supplies and untrimmed hats. The demand in the neighborhood was for the cheap goods which only the wholesalers can produce, not for the higher priced hats made in custom workrooms. Not only in New York City but throughout the country the retail shop is often chiefly a salesroom for hats made at wholesale. Through the millinery jobber the products of wholesale factories of New York are distributed widely among the small owners, who appear to the casual observer to demonstrate the continued survival of the independent hand workers. In reality they are merely adjuncts to the factory system.

Until the present uptown movement began in the wholesale branch of the trade, lower Broadway occupied among wholesalers much the same position as Fifth Avenue holds for retailers. The nearer to Broadway, the more successful the firm. "When people come from out of town to give orders, they go right to Broadway," said one milliner. "They wouldn't bother to go to the shops on the side street. It is better to have your show window on Broadway." Division Street, on the other hand, holds its own distinct place in the trade, serving both retail customers from the lower East Side, and jobbers in search of cheap products for distant states, or for neighborhood shops a few blocks away on Manhattan Island.

As part of the wholesale trade, we discovered evidences of a contract system. For example, on First Street a Russian Jew and his wife have a shop and employ sometimes four workers, sometimes none. They work for several Broadway wholesale firms, trimming cheap ready-to-wear hats. The style which they were making at the time of the visit was a straw hat, trimmed with silk and a single straw buckle, for which the contractor received $2.00 a dozen. In another instance we talked with a milliner whose sister was a contractor for a firm which manufactures a very cheap grade of hat made by hand, of long ribbons of soft straw. Her comment on the contract system was interesting, as presumably she would be in sympathy with the contractor. "Working in a big place for the manufacturer is bad," she said, "but working for a contractor is worse. She is exploited herself by the manufacturer. To make anything she must exploit the girls. They must work for nothing at first, then for $2.00 a week and they never get more than $6.00." The work, of course, is of such cheap grade as to have only a distant resemblance to real millinery. No special skill is needed. The contractor of First Street, to whom we have already referred, said that he and his wife learned the trade in three days. Another, on Allen Street, had been a carpenter, but after a severe illness he became a millinery contractor. He estimated that there were about 12 in the city. Although an exact count would be impossible, it is probable that he underestimated the number, judging by the payroll of one firm investigated by us, which showed at least 12 probable contractors for that one shop. We say "probable" because the line of demarcation between the home worker who has no employes and the contractor who takes on "hands" for the busy season is not very distinct, and cannot be traced on the payroll except through inference from the size of the earnings. One employer told us that the amount of contracting was once much larger in this trade, but that the work was so poorly done and the loss through spoiling materials so serious that the custom had been largely abandoned.

The fact that a woman's hat may be acquired not only in such variety of styles but at so many distinct stages of completion, from the purchase of the materials for its home creation to the buying of a complete structure from a highly organized establishment, indicates that the millinery industry includes more different trades than we imagine when we enter the little shop around the corner. We learned of its many ramifications early in our inquiry through the practical necessity of answering the question: What is the millinery trade, and how much of it must we investigate?

The raw materials of the retailer or the home milliner include either buckram or wire with which to make frames, or else the frames themselves made in another shop; straw hats made by machinery or straw with which to model a hand-made product; silk, ribbon, chiffon, or velvet bought from stores to be made into trimmings, or else the trimmings themselves, chiffon already shirred, or ribbon wired in a millinery supply house; artificial flowers and feathers ready for use, or, more rarely, the materials to make them; and in response to this demand we have straw hat factories, pressed hat manufactories, artificial flower and feather shops, and millinery supply houses, or we have a single large wholesale establishment with a department for each of these divisions of the trade, and all would be called millinery.

The manufacture of pressed hats is a factory industry carried on chiefly by men. Women are extensively employed in machine operating on straw hats, but obviously this work, like the making of flowers and feathers and other trimmings, is very different from that of the milliner who brings together all these products in the final task of trimming. On the other hand, as we have already indicated, in many shops, especially retail, it may be part of the day's work of a real milliner, in the limited and more common sense of the word, to make a hat of velvet instead of using the pressed shape which is a factory product, or to sew together straw by hand, or even to prepare flowers and feathers. While this persistence of hand work makes it difficult to chart or diagram the industry, nevertheless the difference is obvious between manufacturing products used in millinery and trimming hats. It was this task of hat trimming which we chose as the subject of our inquiry, including in this occupation all of the work which milliners, again in the common acceptance of the term, may be called upon to do, such as the making of a frame or the sewing together of straw, even though these processes would be excluded when they were carried on in separate factories or in distinct departments.

Naturally, the organization of the workrooms and the division of processes among the workers differ in different branches of the trade and in different types of shop. To create the artistic and stylish products of the high grade retail shops a careful system of organization is essential, but it must be not the subdivision which results in isolation of workers in one process from those in another, but a group plan whereby the most humble

Some Branches of the Millinery Trade

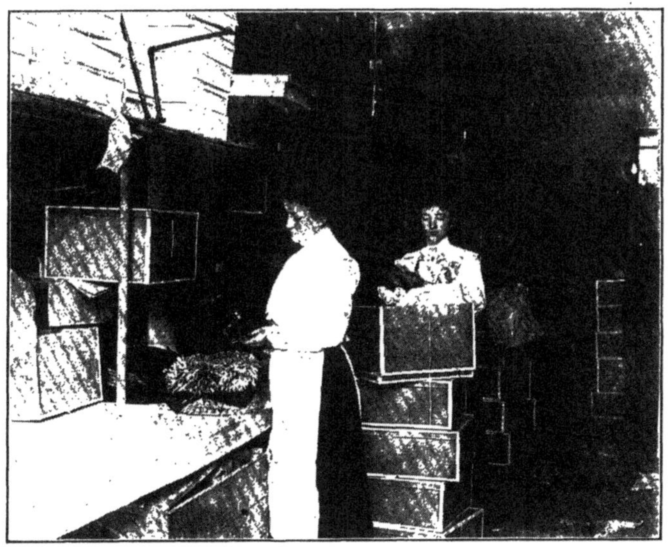

Packing Hats

apprentice can watch and be watched by the best paid trimmer. The designer creates the style. The trimmers are responsible for developing in actual materials the ideas of the designer. Each trimmer has her own corps of assistants, including, generally, an apprentice who makes bandeaux and linings, improvers to shirr chiffon, make folds, and put the linings into the hats, preparers who are a little more expert than improvers but who do essentially the same work, and makers* to construct the frames which shall follow exactly the measurements necessary to create a hat in right proportions, to cover the frames with crinoline, and to prepare the hat in all other particulars for the final work of the trimmer. Neatness and accuracy and delicacy of touch are essential requirements, and no careless worker may stay long in a corps of milliners who produce hats ranging in price from $50 to $150, or more. Often the trimmer has a definite commercial responsibility to make her "table" pay, just as the forewoman or head of a department is charged with the duty of securing an adequate profit on the work which she supervises. In the cheaper grade of retail shops the processes are essentially the same, but designers and highly artistic trimmers are not found in them and the workmanship is less accurate and careful. The "madame" plans the designs after frequent

* These workers are usually called "milliners," but, as this word can be used more conveniently to designate the entire group, we have substituted the less common name of "maker" for the girl whose occupation is here described.

inspection of Fifth Avenue windows and costume magazines, or even after a brief period of employment in an establishment in which the season begins earlier than her own. When a shop becomes a little more prosperous, a trimmer capable of designing hats may be employed for a week or a month at the beginning of the season. As the establishment grows still more prosperous and the number of its employes increases, they are organized into groups with a division of tasks among them.

As an example of the methods of grouping the workers in high grade shops, we may describe one of the most fashionable of the retail establishments. A trimmer or a designer is placed in charge of each table, with six or seven girls working under her direction, including usually one apprentice, two improvers, two expert preparers, and two makers. Sometimes four makers are found in one group, instead of two makers and two preparers. In the busy season six or seven tables or groups of workers are kept busy. Each group is self-sufficient, entirely responsible for the designing and making of the hat from lining to trimming. It follows that an apprentice may get better training at one table than at another according to the skill of the trimmer or designer in supervising the girls for whom she is responsible. So distinct are these groups in some shops that the length of the season may differ from table to table if one trimmer takes a longer vacation than others, or a designer spends a longer or shorter time in Paris.

Table 4 shows the number of each type of worker employed in another retail shop in which this same plan is carried out.

TABLE 4.—DESIGNATION OF OCCUPATIONS OF WOMEN EMPLOYED IN ONE RETAIL MILLINERY ESTABLISHMENT, FEBRUARY 2, 1914

Occupation	Women
Forewoman and assistant forewoman	2
Designer	3
Copyist	5
Maker	63
Improver	5
Apprentice	10
Feather hand	6
Stock girl	1
Errand girl	1
Shopper	1
Total	97

The apprentices numbered approximately one in 10. The makers constituted the largest group, numbering 63, while only five improvers were employed. This was due not to any difference in plan of work as compared with shops employing more equal groups of improvers, preparers, and makers, but was indicative rather of a difference in naming divisions of work. The makers represented a wide range of earnings and experience and a more exact assignment of titles would have placed some of them in the ranks of improvers or preparers. In this shop models are made to be sold to other establishments and these are duplicated; hence the employment of five copyists.

The six "feather hands" prepared the feather trimmings which some other retail shops always purchase from feather manufacturers. The forewoman and her assistant were executives in charge of the workroom, with such duties as engaging workers, attending to orders, marking hats, and keeping account of the cost of materials for each hat. They had not been trained as milliners. The stock girl worked under the direct supervision of the forewoman, taking care of materials used in the workroom. The functions of errand girl, shopper, and designer are sufficiently obvious to require no explanation.

The best of the wholesale milliners create models as distinctive and unique as those to be found in retail shops and the workmanship and shop organization are similar. In other establishments, of cheaper grade, hats are sold by the dozen or the gross, and uniformity in the making is necessary. From this fact arises the need for copyists, workers who can make a hat from frame to trimming, copying exactly the model before them. The more uniform the style, the less is the need for the corps of apprentices, improvers, preparers, makers, trimmers, and designers.

From the uniformity of design develops also a subdivision of processes somewhat like that in clothing shops. In one typical wholesale shop, for instance, in which medium grade "tailored hats" are made, that is, the ready-to-wear type, the workers are divided into distinct groups according to processes. One group cuts out the requisite amount of straw and braid, silk and lining, measuring the amount needed for one hat and then duplicating the parts needed for the total amount of the order for that particular model. The material for each hat is then rolled together and a dozen or more sets given to each worker. Other workers make linings by machine, or tuck or hem materials like chiffon or silk for trimming. Copyists then make the entire hat, duplicating it many times. It will be noted that in such a shop the description of processes already given does not apply, and that new processes, like cutting and machine sewing, must be added to our list. This kind of machine sewing is not the same as the making of straw hats by machine which, although a part of the millinery industry, as we have explained, is not included in the branch of the trade which we have designated as hat trimming. Table 5 shows the distribution of the workroom force in a wholesale establishment.

A little more than two in five are copyists. Cutter,* liner, and machine operator are specialists. The large group of apprentices, preparers, and makers is to be accounted for by the fact that even in the wholesale trade by no means all the hats are of the ready-to-wear type. Many are made by much the same process as in retail shops. It should be understood that the relative importance

* The greater part of the cutting, as well as the frame making in wholesale shops, is usually done by men.

of different processes varies from year to year with changes in the fashion. Especially in wholesale the make-up of the force varies with the comparative demand for hand-made or for blocked or pressed hats. In the winter of 1913–14 hand-made hats were fashionable, and consequently more hand workers were employed.

TABLE 5.—DESIGNATION OF OCCUPATIONS OF WOMEN EMPLOYED IN ONE WHOLESALE MILLINERY ESTABLISHMENT, FEBRUARY 7, 1914

Occupation	Women
Forewoman	2
Designer	2
Trimmer	1
Copyist	46
Maker	36
Preparer	4
Apprentice	4
Cutter	2
Liner	1
Machine operator	2
Stock girl	7
Total	107

It should be observed that the subdivision of processes which we have described as characteristic of certain wholesale factories is radically different from the division of work in a retail shop or in a wholesale establishment where high grade hats are made. In the retail shops the workers are grouped together in the making of one hat. In the typical cheap wholesale workroom the parts of the hat are divided between separate groups of workers. The

A Small Retail Shop
Each hat is different

Copyists in a Broadway Wholesale Shop

difference is fundamental. The latter plan results in specialization. The former means that each worker in the group has the advantage of watching every other part of the hat trimming, and increase in experience leads to more and more responsibility. The maker differs from the preparer and the preparer from an improver rather in length of experience and adaptability than in type of work, and every maker must have been first an apprentice, then an improver, then a preparer, or at least have had an equivalent experience even if she did not have these titles.

Whether the number of workers engaged in the various tasks in these two shops is typical of others in the same branches of the trade may best be determined by Table 6, showing the distribution of the workers in occupational groups in the shops in which we studied the payrolls. The table is compiled from the records of employes actually at work at the time of investigation.

Approximately half the workers in wholesale shops were copyists, while in retail the makers numbered a little less than half the total group. The proportion of apprentices was about one in 10 in retail and only about one in 35 in wholesale. All the figures in the table, however, must be used cautiously. The description already given shows how loose is the definition of terms. Workers called by the same name have different duties in different types of shops and even in different shops of the same type. Workers with the same duties

TABLE 6.—OCCUPATIONS OF WOMEN EMPLOYED IN 29 RETAIL AND 27 WHOLESALE MILLINERY ESTABLISHMENTS, AS SHOWN BY CURRENT PAY-ROLL. 1914

Occupation	Women employed in		All women
	Retail shops	Wholesale shops	
Forewoman	10	20	30
Assistant forewoman	4	5	9
Designer	27	45	72
Trimmer	15	62	77
Copyist	34	702	736
Maker	258	72	330
Preparer	19	270	289
Improver	62	16	78
Apprentice	56	41	97
Machine operator	..	72	72
Stock and floor girl	20	31	51
Feather and flower hand	24	3	27
Cutter	..	21	21
Crown sewer	..	11	11
Errand girl	6	5	11
Crimper	..	9	9
Shopper	7	2	9
Packer	..	7	7
Straw sewer	..	5	5
Wire-frame maker	..	4	4
Helper	3	..	3
Liner	1	1	2
Examiner	..	1	1
Total	546	1,405	1,951

have different names. It is doubtful whether each of the 27 designers, so called in 29 retail shops, deserved the title. It is certain that the trimmer in a little neighborhood shop resembles only in name the woman responsible for the commercial success of a table of workers in a Fifth Avenue shop. Still less would be the resemblance of some of those called trimmers in wholesale shops. For example, one manufacturer of hats which are but slightly trimmed declared that the trimmers in his shop were not even milliners. "Anybody who can handle a needle can do our work," he said. "In a place like J——'s (naming a wholesale shop) or in a retail shop they would spend half a day trimming a hat that we trim in five minutes. It is entirely different work." In one retail establishment we were told that the trimmers were the designers, and, the employer added, "Sometimes a trimmer does not know how to make a hat at all. She is expected merely to design it."

Many employers complained of the scarcity of designers with original ideas. Many of them will do well for a few days and after that they have no new suggestions to make, showing that at first their success was due rather to remembering models seen in other shops. Some firms follow the practice of changing their designers more or less frequently in their search for new ideas. In one Fifth Avenue shop we were told that they employed no designer, and that they prefer to get their models from Paris. This use of models is illustrated also by the practice of employing a designer for a brief period to make a certain specified number of hats, which then become patterns for the trimmers. As in every other position in the trade, the duties of the workers vary from shop to shop.

Variety in the type of shop is reflected in the

unsatisfactory state of official statistics about millinery. In 1900, in the United States census of manufactures, 517 custom millinery establishments were counted in New York City, employing 2,723 women, 88 men and 25 children under sixteen years.* Since that date "millinery custom work" has been omitted from the manufacturing census as more properly a hand industry than a manufacturing pursuit. The wholesale millinery trade is counted under the heading of "millinery and lace goods," which was defined in 1910 as including hand-made muslin and lace curtains; dress, cloak, and millinery trimmings; embroideries and crocheted goods; hat and bonnet frames; ladies' belts, collars, neckwear, and handkerchiefs; hats, trimmed and untrimmed; laces; plaiting and puffs; ruching and ruffing, and veilings.† One is reminded of the etymologist's attempt to derive the word milliner from *mille* (thousand), "as having a thousand small wares to sell."‡ The number of workers employed in the manufacture of these diverse products in New York in 1910 was 20,561,§ of whom 16,097‖ were women. It should be noted

* Twelfth United States Census, 1900. Manufactures, Part II, Vol. VIII, p. 626.

† Thirteenth United States Census, 1910. Abstract with Supplement for New York, p. 693.

‡ Encyclopædia Britannica, 11th Edition, Vol. XVIII, p. 468.

§ Thirteenth United States Census, 1910. Manufactures, Vol. IX, p. 888.

‖ The average number of female wage-earners, sixteen years and over, employed in millinery and lace goods was 15,865. The 284 wage-earners in this industry who were under sixteen are not separated according to sex in the census table. On the same page, how-that not only is the group too inclusive to serve as a measure of the number of milliners, but also that some employers in large wholesale millinery establishments are makers of artificial flowers or feathers or other allied products, and their inclusion is another objection to the use of these statistics as a background for our study.

For these reasons the most valuable census information for our purposes is to be found not in the volume on manufactures but in the occupational statistics. These are gathered in the house-to-house enumeration of the population, when schedules are filled calling for a statement of the occupation of every member of the family. The number thus reporting themselves as milliners is undoubtedly a better index of the size of the trade than the inclusive group statistics given in the manufacturing census. The occupational data in the census of 1910 showed* in Greater New York 12,096 women and girls listed as "milliners and millinery dealers," and 1,825 as "apprentices to dressmakers and milliners." As about half† of these appren-

ever, figures are given showing the number of males and females under sixteen employed in this industry on December 15 or the nearest representative day. The proportion of females on this one day was taken as a basis for estimating the average number of females under sixteen. According to this ratio, the average number of female wage-earners under sixteen was 232, giving a total of 16,097 women employed in millinery and lace goods.

* Thirteenth United States Census, 1910. Population, Vol. IV. Occupation Statistics, p. 574.

† Since for the entire United States the number of apprentices for dressmakers is about the same as for milliners (Ibid., p. 312), it may be assumed that the same proportion holds for both New York City and Manhattan.

tices were probably milliners, the total number was approximately 13,000 as compared with 1,470 men "milliners and millinery dealers."* No men or boys were listed as apprentices in millinery. Thus, in the whole group of about 14,500 the proportion of men was a little more than 10 per cent. In Manhattan† the number of women milliners, including about half the group of apprentices to dressmakers and milliners, was about 7,700, and the number of men 1,020, a total of over 8,700 milliners, or three-fifths of the number in that occupation in all the boroughs of the city. Apparently the number has increased rapidly since 1900, when 7,651 women and 357 men were recorded in the census as milliners in New York.‡ From 8,000 to 14,500 is an increase of about 80 per cent.

The industrial directory published in 1912 by the New York State Department of Labor gave us the most recent information regarding the millinery trade.§ In the city of New York 860 milli-

* Ibid., p. 572.

† Ibid., pp. 575–76.

‡ Twelfth United States Census, 1900. Occupations, pp. 638 and 640. The inclusion of "millinery dealers" in the census of 1910 may account for a small part of this increase.

§ These figures, also, must be used with caution in a discussion of the millinery trade, for the list of millinery establishments in the industrial directory included also firms engaged in the making of shapes of straw, felt, wool, silk, fiber, or other material, as well as hats for children, and feathers and flowers produced in departments of millinery establishments. Moreover, in more than one instance employers listed in this group manufactured gowns as well as hats, and the report of their number of employes included both dressmakers and milliners. It would be impossible without investigation to eliminate these allied occupations from the list and count only the milliners.

nery establishments were counted, employing a shop force of 11,837, of whom 2,952 were men and boys, and 8,885 women and girls.* In Manhattan the number of shops was 628,† with a force of 2,837 men and boys and 7,933 women and girls, or 10,770 in all. In Brooklyn the total shop force was only 872, and the combined number in the three other boroughs was but 195. These directory figures show the concentration of important firms in Manhattan and indicate why it seemed wise to limit our investigation to that borough. It should be noted that as the occupational statistics of the census are based on a home enumeration, they tell us nothing about the location of workshops. Milliners listed in Brooklyn may be working in a Fifth Avenue shop in Manhattan. Thus, although according to the census only three-fifths of the milliners lived in Manhattan, according to the labor department directory 91 per cent worked there. Since ours was a study of shops, not of homes, the directory figures were the correct guide for us.‡

* New York State Department of Labor. Industrial Directory, 1912, Table XI, p. cxcix.

† Only 160 of these were important enough to list by name and address, while 468 were classed as "small factories." Ibid., p. 334. In Brooklyn only six shops were listed by name (Ibid., p. 149), and in the other three boroughs no milliner attained that distinction.

‡ Since our inquiry was completed, the 1913 volume has been issued. It shows smaller numbers in millinery than the preceding year. There were in 1913 in New York City 542 shops employing a total shop force of 11,726, of whom 3,829 were men and 7,897 women. For Manhattan the figures are 441 shops employing 10,601 workers, of whom 3,444 were men and 7,157 women. The apparent decrease since 1912 may be due to an incomplete census, another illustration

No state in the Union is without milliners but none has as many as New York. Between Alaska with six and New York state with more than 22,500, the variety in numbers is great.* New York state's nearest competitor is Pennsylvania, with nearly 12,500. Illinois has third place with approximately 11,000. Of all the cities of 25,000 or more listed in the census,† none is without milliners,‡ but New York City is in the lead with 14,500, with Chicago second, employing about 6,500, Philadelphia third, with 4,000, and St. Louis fourth, with 2,300. The total number throughout the country is approximately 134,000.§ Thus it will be seen that the concentration in any one city is not marked, compared with other industries which tend to grow especially in one locality.

A wide distribution would seem to imply local consumption and, as a matter of fact, the local milliner does undoubtedly serve her own community. She draws on the large cities, however, both for models and for supplies, and New York sells not only to New Yorkers but caters to a market extending from Maine to Texas. The

of the difficulty of securing exact statistics about millinery. The increase of men as compared with the decrease of women may be due to the inclusion of more shops of the factory type in 1913 and fewer shops where hand work predominated. (New York State Department of Labor, Industrial Directory, 1913. Table VI, p. 103.)

* Thirteenth United States Census, 1910. Population, Vol. IV, Occupation Statistics, pp. 96 ff. Includes "milliners and millinery dealers" and half the number of "dressmakers' and milliners' apprentices." (See last footnote, p. 53.)

† Ibid., pp. 152–291.

‡ Includes apprentices.

§ Ibid., pp. 91–92.

wider the market the more complicated its method of organization. In millinery especially, the wide separation between the designer and the probable wearer of the hat introduces an element of chance which contributes in no small degree to the irregularity of the seasons. New York waits for reports from distant states as to the demands of the customers and the way a new fashion "takes," while the rest of the country looks to New York for information on the newest styles. It is no wonder that to trim hats in dull season to be sold later seems to employers a wholly unnecessary business risk.

For those who wish to see the seasons prolonged, the possibility of a better organization of the process of selling, which would imply a more even distribution of orders throughout the year, is of prime importance from this point of view. The decentralized character of the trade is a discouraging factor. Moreover, it is difficult to determine whether the tendency is toward concentration in a few large establishments or distribution in many small shops. In machine processes the larger establishment has advantages. In hand-work variety and diversity in design are assets, and this fact gives encouragement to many independent milliners. On the other hand, reputation, which is important in getting one's designs accepted, is so dependent upon fashionable location and resources to pay large salaries to designers and to make frequent pilgrimages to Paris, that even in the hand processes which in themselves can be successfully accomplished by one worker without assistants, the firm with capital will acquire a larger and larger share of orders. The small neighborhood shop tends to become a distributing center for the wholesale factories, performing the task of the middleman, with one or two milliners to adapt the style to the taste of individual customers. This is significant, since the persistence of the small shop may indicate not the probability that millinery will continue to be thoroughly decentralized and unorganized, but merely that the institution of the middleman is flourishing in the industry. Meanwhile, whatever the tendency may be, we have to deal now with a diversified occupation in which orders and, consequently, permanence of employment are dependent upon a disorganized system of buying and selling, with keen competition and elements of luck more powerful than any present efforts to develop a scientific plan of meeting market demands.

CHAPTER III

THE WORKERS

IT WOULD be untrue to characterize the milliners of New York by any statements which would imply that they are a homogeneous group. Differences in age, in nationality, in qualifications, in economic status are marked, and any common characteristics other than employment in the same occupation would be difficult to find. Indeed, it is doubtful whether any other industry can show a greater variety economically and personally than exists in the millinery trade. Our visits took us to the home of a designer with earnings large enough to be subject to the income tax, and to two tiny rooms where the milliner's small earnings and the board paid by her aunt were the only means of support for her sick mother and herself. We talked with a married woman whose husband owned two houses and a saloon, but who preferred to work in a shop because she was lonely at home. We found two or three instances of "pin-money workers," who so described themselves; as, for example, the girl who had been at home for nearly a year after learning her trade in a retail shop, and who said that she had not really been obliged to work and that now her mother needed her at home. Her father and three brothers were in the automobile business, and their income was quite sufficient for the support of the family. In another case, a young woman who also described herself as a "pin-money worker" was earning 50 cents a week as an apprentice in a Fifth Avenue shop, having chosen this method of learning an occupation which she regarded as an accomplishment. Far more typical was the family in which a high standard was maintained through the employment of the daughters as well as the sons. The father was a mechanic, and the three daughters, one a dressmaker, one a milliner, and one in a novelty factory, were all at work. The mother who, before the girls were old enough to work, contributed to their income by dressmaking and finishing clothing, now keeps house and makes all the girls' clothes, including their coats and suits. They are all alert and ambitious, and it is in no dilettante spirit but in downright earnestness that the girls are doing their share to maintain the family standard. Equally typical, though much less cheerful, was a family of five, consisting of the mother, the father who did tailoring work at home, a son employed in a clothing store, a daughter in school, and the milliner, who earned only $6.00 a week. "She cannot be idle even in dull season," said her mother. "She must work. My husband is old and cannot work much and we have the rent to pay. When it gets slack in one place she must find another."

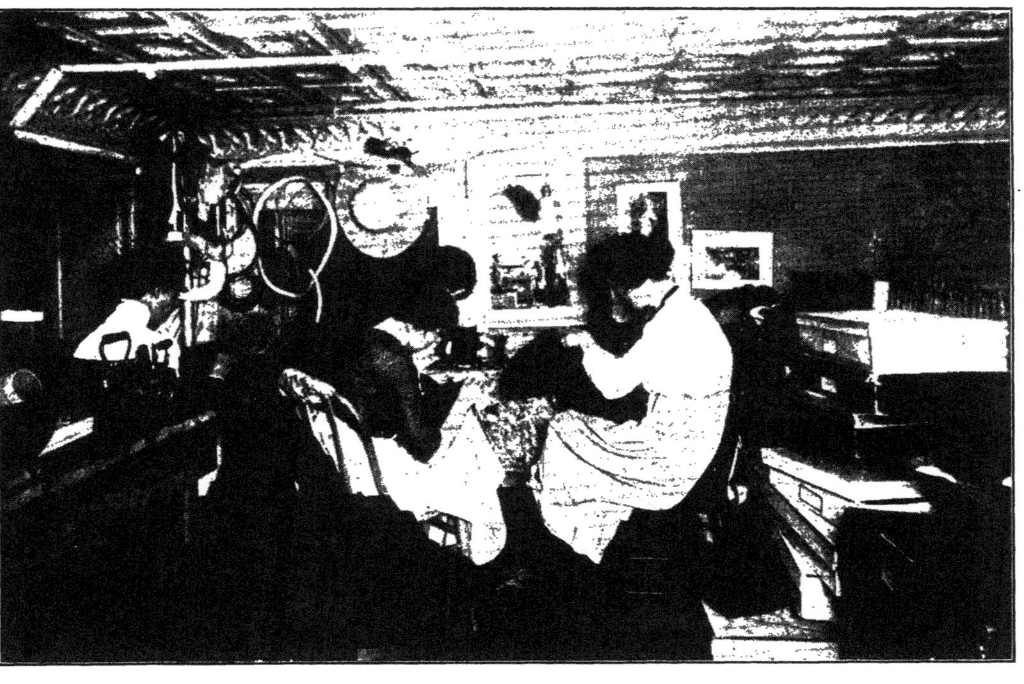

Working on a Balcony above the Store

It is certainly safe to say that, however much the family stories may differ in detail, in the large majority of households withdrawal of the milliner's earnings means dispensing, perforce, with some of the necessities of living. Further evidence on this point belongs in the discussion of wages. The important fact to note here is that the amateurish worker who is a wage-earner, not through necessity but through a superficial kind of choice, does exist, but is merely an incident in the industry and not to be confused with the girl whose home is comfortable but whose work is, nevertheless, necessary to maintain or to improve the traditional family standard. These standards may differ widely, however, among milliners even in the same shop, a fundamental fact which deserves further emphasis in the discussion of wage rates.

The variety in family standards represented in the trade is due in part to the diversity of conditions already noted between shop and shop, but more, perhaps, to the enviable position which millinery holds among occupations, so that love of the work as well as the need for earnings may be a factor in a milliner's employment. The hope of having one's own business some day lures on the young worker who would otherwise be discouraged by low pay and short seasons, and this prospect is something for which we have found the family also willing to make sacrifices. Furthermore, it is, as one of the girls said, "an interesting trade.

It cultivates your mind, makes you think, and gives you new ideas." Others, less analytical, merely described it as a trade with "a nice name," employing a "refined class of girls." It attracts young girls just leaving school, who look upon wage-earning as part of the natural course of events, and it is likely to be selected also by women of the so-called "leisure class" when they are suddenly and unexpectedly forced to earn their own living. Thus it draws together workers of diverse social experiences.

We were interested especially in the owners of the small neighborhood shops and their careers. We wanted to know how they had happened to become independent milliners, and what had been their preparation. A woman on Third Avenue had started her business three years before, with experience in buying but none in millinery. It was her opinion that to know how to buy was more important than to know how to trim, for unwise buying can very soon bankrupt the business. An Austrian woman on the lower East Side had her store on the ground floor of the tenement in which she lived. She had been in business for herself for fourteen years, after only two years' experience as a milliner in America. She had learned the trade in Austria. "There it is for nice work," she said. "Here it is all for hurry up." On upper Broadway we found a newly organized shop whose owner had been a designer earning $50 a week, honored occasionally by being sent abroad to buy models in Paris. She was confident that in another year she would earn more working independently than as a designer for someone else. The owner of a forlorn little shop in a tenement on Columbus Avenue had learned her trade in one of the best of the Fifth Avenue shops, and had then begun to acquire customers of her own by making over their hats. She has succeeded well enough to have been an independent milliner for four years, but she has neither space nor capital for a supply of hats trimmed in advance and can only take orders, having the customers, if possible, supply their own materials.

A more prosperous milliner had learned her trade in a small Pennsylvania town, and after experience in a wholesale shop in New York and a season in a western city, she had opened her own shop in New York ten years ago; she had moved three times, each move representing an advance in her status in the trade. She declared that it was easier to be successful in one's own business in New York than in a smaller place. In her opinion, the one essential for success in New York is to be able to pay rent in a fashionable location. In contrast, another milliner had moved farther away from Fifth Avenue in order to be in a neighborhood where cash is paid. Her Fifth Avenue charge customers had been a cause of much anxiety. "If a milliner has anything left for herself at the end of the season," she said, "she is doing well. Rent, materials, and wages are all so expensive. No one can get along on millinery alone. They are all selling waists and dresses now."

Of course, not all the shops which display a sign with the name of "Lillian" or "Therese" really belong to Therese or Lillian. They are controlled by others, and the fiction of ownership by "madam," who may in reality be only the head trimmer or the manager, is a concession to the shopping ladies who like to buy hats "from my little French milliner who makes hats just to suit me, and has her own shop just around the corner." It is not without interest to note that many retail shops are run in the names of women, but that practically all the wholesale establishments display men's names on their signs, whereas in both branches of the trade it is very common for a husband and wife to manage the business together. Where this kind of family partnership does not exist, it seems still necessary in the most successful enterprises to have the work of management divided between men and women.

The majority of the women workers in the trade in New York are young,—younger than dressmakers and about the same age as saleswomen,—according to the United States census of 1910. Of the milliners, 42 per cent were under twenty-one, compared with 21 per cent of the dressmakers and 40 per cent of the saleswomen.* The data gathered in connection with the payroll study for the

* Thirteenth United States Census, 1910. Population, Vol. IV. Occupation Statistics, p. 574.

Factory Investigating Commission showed about the same proportion of young workers—40 per cent under twenty-one. Only a little more than 1 per cent were under sixteen, due partly, no doubt, to the failure of some of the young people to make a truthful statement, but chiefly to the fact that, because of the law limiting the hours of work of children to eight in a day, and because of some rigid requirements with reference to work certificates, it is becoming the practice not to employ any girls under sixteen.

Only a very small proportion, 5 per cent, were married, 3 per cent were widowed or divorced, and 92 per cent were single, as one might naturally expect from the youth of the workers. It should be recalled that this group was made up chiefly of employes in the larger shops. Among the owners of small enterprises the proportion of married women would probably be larger.

Diversity in nationality is not surprising in any industry in New York City. A handful of records taken at random from the file showed, in succession, an Italian who had been in New York since she was eight years old, a Russian, a Roumanian, a New Englander from a country town who works in the city once a year to learn the new styles, a real New Yorker of English parentage, the daughter of an Austrian from Budapest, the American-born daughter of a Frenchman, a woman born in India of French parents, a German who had been a milliner in Baden, an Irish girl who had learned her trade in Dublin, and a Canadian who had thought that New York offered better opportunities to a milliner than she could find in her own home. Of the 252 girls whom we interviewed at home, as many as 26 had learned the trade in foreign lands, in Russia, England, Ireland, Germany, Austria-Hungary, Sweden, Italy, Roumania, and France. The proportion of foreign born differs greatly, however, in the two main branches of the trade, as Table 7 shows.

TABLE 7.—NATIVITY OF WOMEN EMPLOYED IN RETAIL AND WHOLESALE MILLINERY ESTABLISHMENTS, AS SHOWN BY CURRENT PAYROLL. 1914

Country of birth	Women employed in		All women	
	Retail shops	Wholesale shops	Number	Per cent
United States	374	417	791	58.6
Foreign countries	95	464	559	41.4
Russia	14	224	238	17.6
Austria-Hungary	5	79	84	6.2
Italy	6	44	50	3.7
Germany	19	26	45	3.3
Roumania	4	34	38	2.8
England	10	16	26	1.9
France	14	10	24	1.8
Ireland	3	8	11	.8
Sweden	6	4	10	.8
Other countries [a]	14	19	33	2.5
Total	469	881	1,350[b]	100.0

[a] Includes Canada, Belgium, Argentine Republic, Australia, Bulgaria, Denmark, Holland, Norway, Palestine, Scotland, Spain, Switzerland, and the West Indies.

[b] Of the 1,363 women who supplied personal records, 13 did not state country of birth, although six of these indicated that they were foreign born.

About 59 per cent of the women who filled our record cards were native born. In wholesale shops the proportion of foreign born was 53 per cent, and in retail only 20 per cent. The largest single group were Russians, most of them Jews, of whom many had come here because of persecution at home. Twenty-one other countries were represented. In the smaller group, interviewed at home, the number of native born exactly equalled the foreigners and, as in the figures already quoted, the natives predominated in retail establishments and the foreigners in wholesale. Only about one in nine of the native born, however, was of native parentage. One, a daughter of a German, was quite sure that the trouble with the trade was the number of immigrants in it, and she favored exclusion of foreigners. Another, with ideas on immigration, told us that her mother came from Germany more than sixty years before on a sailing vessel, and went to work in a shirt factory where she used a sewing machine of the first type ever made. Her hours were from 7 a. m. to 6 p. m., and her wages $2.00 a week. She had lived for thirty-six years in the same street and had watched the coming first of the Jews and then of the Italians who finish clothing at home all day long. She grieved over what seemed to her the deterioration of the neighborhood.

As to the effect of the employment of foreigners on the millinery trade, no satisfactory evidence could be gathered. The fact is that so little cohesion exists among milliners that no one group can be said to have had any real influence except by accident. Employers had ideas as to the comparative skill of workers of different nationalities. We were told that the French are born with a knowledge of millinery and that an American can never equal them; that European girls have more interest and talent, while "Americans care more for work with the pen than with the needle"; that the Italians are quiet and thorough, while the Russians Jews are often a disturbing element. It was among the Russians that the movement to organize a trade union* originated a few years ago, and unsuccessful as were their efforts, the few employers who knew of their existence were still so afraid of them that they looked askance at the agents of the Factory Investigating Commission, fearing lest an inquiry into conditions of labor should encourage the Russian workers to renewed agitation.

On both sides of the industrial bargain much discontent was expressed. Employers complained of the irresponsibility of the workers, their tendency to give up jobs at inconvenient seasons for no good reason, their lack of ambition or appreciation of small kindnesses on the part of their superior officers. The girls complained that their employers showed them no consideration, saved money whenever possible by laying them off without warning, and made no effort to advance them

* See p. 134.

in work or wages unless the workers themselves protested. One girl expressed a not uncommon sentiment when she told how her employer discovered that she had good taste and so sent her out to buy the hat shapes, when experience in the shop was what she wanted, and she added, "I tell you, it does not pay to show too much what you can do. They take advantage of you."

Each side, indeed, seems to be afraid that the other will take some undue advantage, an attitude which may be only human but which is certainly an important factor in industrial relations in many trades besides millinery. The discontent is individual, however; and although it is evident to an investigator that the workers have much in common in experience and ideas, a sense of membership in a group or conception of possible group action seems absolutely lacking. As a woman prominent in efforts to organize trade unions among women expressed it, "You might as well try to direct the wind as to organize milliners." Undoubtedly the short seasons, the brief terms of employment in any one shop, the changes in personnel each season, as well as the youth of the workers, their diverse social experiences and their varied inheritances from many different nations, account for the characteristic condition of an industry in which the workers are a chance collection of individuals rather than a group of fellow-employes with common aims and an explicitly recognized community of interests.

CHAPTER IV

THE SEASONS

UNEMPLOYMENT is the most important fact in the occupation of being a milliner. Twice a year more than half the workers in the trade are laid off because the short season is over. In some years when a general industrial depression affects millinery in common with all other industries, the period of employment may be shorter than usual or the number employed fewer, even in the busy months. The milliner may also lose time because of sickness, or because she is dissatisfied with wages or hours and thinks a change would be desirable, or because she is unsatisfactory to the trimmer, or because the weather has been bad and the sale of hats less brisk, or because her employer lacked capital or good business judgment and consequently failed, or because the fashions changed and the demand for hand-work was reduced in comparison with machine-made products. The causes of irregularity are many, some of them common to all industries, and others peculiar to millinery. Whatever the cause, however, the effect of loss of time on wages is serious, and a full understanding of it is necessary to a comprehension of the facts about wages, which were the center of interest in this investigation.

What the girls told us about the great difficulty of supporting themselves when work and income were so irregular, and what the employers said of the trials of running a business in which the market was so fickle, were fully corroborated in the payrolls. The investigators repeated the same experience in shop after shop, finding the list of names comparatively short in the first week in January, noting gradual additions week by week until all the vacant spaces were filled, and then a rapid subtraction of one name after another until a mere fraction of the force remained. That this was not a mere impression in a few shops was shown in the final count of the workers and the sum of their wages week by week in all the establishments* studied. The facts are pictured in the two accompanying diagrams.

It will be recalled that some of the larger retail shops have also some wholesale trade. These we have classified in these diagrams and in some subsequent tables as retail-wholesale. In earlier tables these retail-wholesale shops have been included in the retail group. The diagram shows that the peak of employment in these establishments precedes the maximum in other retail shops, that the fluctuation is not quite so great, and that the pe-

* Some of the detailed statistics of irregular employment and wages on which statements in this and the following chapter are based will be found in the Supplementary Report, pp. 197 ff.

riod of minimum employment does not last so long. This seems to indicate some slight advantage in the larger establishments in regularity of work.

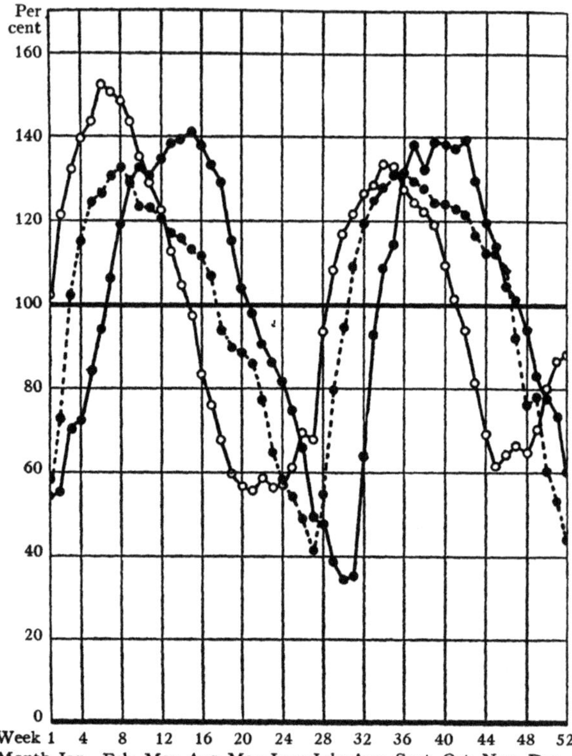

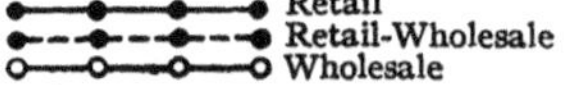

DIAGRAM I.—WOMEN EMPLOYED IN RETAIL, RETAIL-WHOLESALE, AND WHOLESALE MILLINERY ESTABLISHMENTS IN EACH WEEK OF THE YEAR 1913, AS PERCENTAGES OF THE ANNUAL AVERAGES

Nevertheless, in all the branches of the trade the variations in the force are very great.

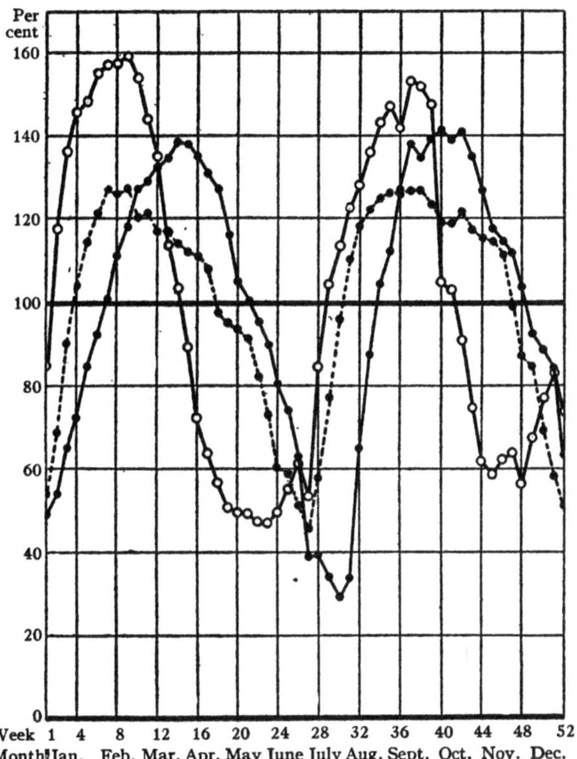

DIAGRAM 2.—TOTAL WAGES PAID IN RETAIL, RETAIL-WHOLESALE, AND WHOLESALE MILLINERY ESTABLISHMENTS IN EACH WEEK OF THE YEAR 1913, AS PERCENTAGES OF THE ANNUAL AVERAGES

In plotting the diagrams the average for the fifty-two weeks was indicated as 100 per cent, and the rise in busy season and the fall in dull season

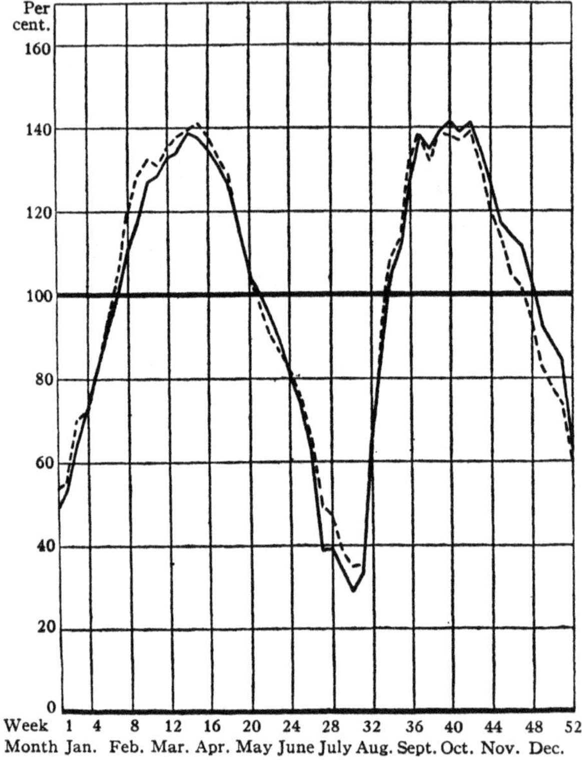

DIAGRAM 3.—WOMEN EMPLOYED AND TOTAL WAGES PAID IN RETAIL MILLINERY ESTABLISHMENTS IN EACH WEEK OF THE YEAR 1913, AS PERCENTAGES OF THE ANNUAL AVERAGES

measured with reference to this average. The data show that the proportion at work in the dullest week is only 55 per cent of the average force

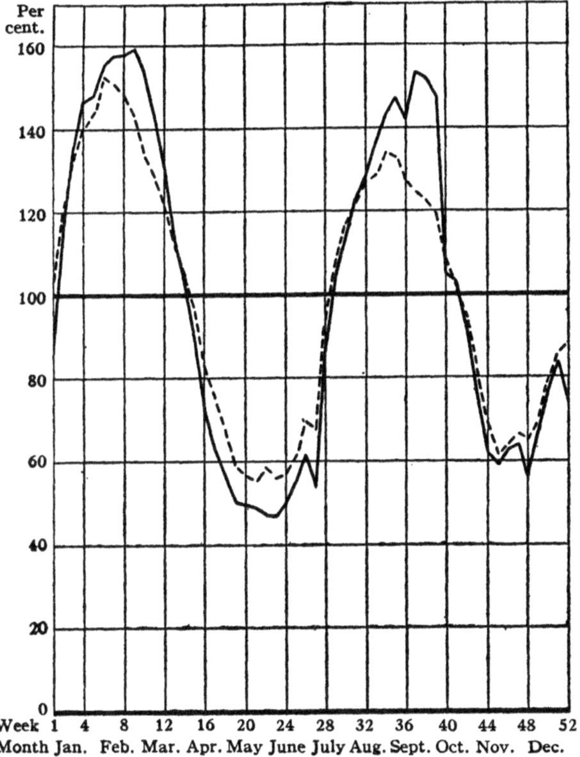

DIAGRAM 4.—WOMEN EMPLOYED AND TOTAL WAGES PAID IN WHOLESALE MILLINERY ESTABLISHMENTS IN EACH WEEK OF THE YEAR 1913, AS PERCENTAGES OF THE ANNUAL AVERAGES

in wholesale, 41 per cent in retail-wholesale, and 35 per cent in retail. The total wages showed a greater variation than the number of employes in the wholesale shops, ranging from 159 per cent to 47 per cent, apparently indicating either that the less well-paid employes were retained in the week of least employment, or that the earnings were reduced. Piece workers often stay in wholesale shops during a dull season, earning very little but still being counted in the number of employes. This is an important factor in causing the wages in wholesale shops to vary more than the number of workers. The reverse was true in retail-wholesale shops, in which the minimum total of wages paid in any one week was 46 per cent of the average, a larger proportion than was shown for the number of employes retained. In wholesale, the week of maximum employment, measured in number of employes, occurred in the first week in February, and the minimum in May; in retail, the maximum week was in April and the minimum the end of July, while retail-wholesale came between the two, with the maximum in the latter half of February and the minimum in the first week of July.

Besides the very large proportion of workers laid off in dull season, these figures reveal the very important fact that millinery has two busy seasons in a year and the majority of milliners must face unemployment twice in twelve months. As it is not by any means certain that one may return in the autumn to the same shop where one worked in the spring, this recurrence of the dull season twice in a year means that many milliners must hunt for jobs four times between Christmas and Christmas, twice in millinery and twice in other occupations, if it is necessary to earn wages continuously.

It is frequently said in the trade that continuous employment is possible by working first in wholesale and then in retail. The diagram shows how limited is this possibility. It is true that the peak of the season in wholesale precedes the peak in retail by several weeks, but after the sixteenth week in the spring and the forty-second week, which occurs in the autumn, the decline is rapid in all branches of the trade. Only for a brief period in both seasons is retail expanding while wholesale is declining. If the total figures for all three branches be considered, we find that in the twenty-seventh week the number employed is but 42 per cent of the maximum, so that at that date 58 in every 100 needed for the maximum week could find no work in either wholesale or retail millinery shops. Moreover, in the last eight weeks of the year the proportion employed never exceeded 57 per cent of the maximum reached in the spring, leaving 43 in every 100 without any place in the workrooms. Additional evidence as to the time when milliners may expect their services to be most in demand is given in Table 8.

TABLE 8.—TIME OF YEAR WHEN THE MAXIMUM FORCE OF WOMEN WAS EMPLOYED IN RETAIL, RETAIL-WHOLESALE, AND WHOLESALE ESTABLISHMENTS. 1913

Time of year	Establishments whose maximum force was employed at some time in the specified months			
	Retail	Retail-wholesale	Wholesale	All establishments
January to March .	2	3	12	17
April to June . .	2	..	..	2
July to September .	5	4	9	18
October to December .	3	..	..	3
Total	12	7	21	40

Two firms employed their maximum force some time in the second quarter (April, May, or June), and three in the fourth quarter (October, November, or December). For all the others investigated, the busiest week occurred in the first or the third quarter. These facts, of course, give no indication of the duration of the seasons, but merely show the time when the largest force was at work. Both individual firm records and their combined totals show that the absolute maximum occurred but once, although the decline following it and the rise preceding it were gradual. To determine the length of the seasons, we have ascertained the number of weeks in which the force was over 90 per cent of the maximum and, to apply a more liberal measure, we have repeated the process for a force of 75 per cent or more. Table 9 shows the facts.

TABLE 9.—WEEKS OF EMPLOYMENT OF MAXIMUM FORCE OF WOMEN IN RETAIL, RETAIL-WHOLESALE, AND WHOLESALE MILLINERY ESTABLISHMENTS. 1913

Branch of trade	Weeks in which number of women employed in each branch of the trade was over	
	90 per cent of maximum force employed in any one week	75 per cent of maximum force employed in any one week
Retail . . .	18	25
Retail-wholesale .	19	31
Wholesale . .	6	21
Total . . .	11	25

During only eleven weeks in the fifty-two was the force in all branches of the trade over 90 per cent of the maximum, and for only twenty-five weeks, less than half the year, was it equal to 75 per cent or more of the number employed at the height of the season. The seasons are longest in retail-wholesale, and shortest in wholesale. These facts as to the duration of the period of employment and the data showing how small a proportion of the force is retained when the season is over, give some realization of how large a number of milliners are necessarily held in reserve in dull season to be ready to fill the workrooms when the demand is at its height.

Comparison with the other industries investigated at the same time by the Factory Investigating Commission shows that fluctuations in the labor force are not peculiar to the millinery trade.

In 18 of the largest department stores of New York City the combined force in 1913 varied from 35,322 in summer to 55,587 before Christmas, while the normal number was reported as 41,828.* Thus the minimum was 64 per cent of the maximum, and the normal force 75 per cent of the largest number employed. Apparently a larger proportion of sales girls than of milliners is retained in dull season, but the relation of the average force to the maximum is not very different. In paper box factories, including those in other parts of the state as well as in New York, the variation in number of employes was much less, from 9,400 to 10,400, but the wages paid in the New York City factories oscillated from $10,000 to $15,000 in a few weeks.† Candy manufacturers in New York City employed 9,700 workers in November, 1912, and 7,100 in July, 1913, while the wages paid dropped from $79,000 in December to $52,600 in July.‡ Nevertheless, although all three of these industries are irregular, none shows as wide variations in employment as the millinery trade.

Great as are these fluctuations, however, they afford but a partial measure of irregularity of employment, for they take no account of changes in the personnel of the force, or the length of employment of individuals in one shop in the course of the year.

* New York State Factory Investigating Commission, Fourth Report, 1915. Vol. II, p. 92.

† Ibid., p. 252.

‡ Ibid., pp. 321–2.

At the Height of the Season

Perhaps the most significant truth revealed in the payroll study is the fact that of all the milliners employed in the shops in the course of the year, only 2.8 per cent received pay for fifty-two weeks. Only 7.6 per cent were employed more than forty-eight weeks. As many as 40 per cent appeared on the payroll four weeks or less in the calendar year. Some of this group may have worked during the preceding year and left soon after New Year's Day, or they may have been engaged in December and continued to work after the period included in the study, but obviously every job lasting less than fifty-two weeks represents either a termination of employment, whether for a temporary period or permanently, or a new engagement, and although the data do not show the total length of employment of individuals, they do show the frequency of breaks in the labor force. Finally, if from Table 1 (p. 11) it be remembered that the total maximum force in the shops investigated was 2,550, the fact that 3,983 individuals appeared on the payrolls in the year indicates the frequent changes in personnel. To be obliged to engage nearly 4,000 workers when the maximum force was 2,550 is an added indication of waste in the organization of employment in millinery. That the shifting of the force is not confined to any one group of workers is shown in Table 10, in which the length of time on the payroll is recorded for the various occupations in millinery workrooms.

TABLE 10.—WEEKS ON PAYROLL, IN ONE POSITION LASTING MORE THAN ONE WEEK DURING THE YEAR 1913, BY OCCUPATIONS, FOR WOMEN EMPLOYED IN MILLINERY ESTABLISHMENTS[a]

Occupation	Women who appeared on the payroll of a single shop during the year 1913							All women	Median number of weeks on payroll during 1913[b]
	More than 1 week and less than 6	6 weeks and less than 10	10 weeks and less than 20	20 weeks and less than 30	30 weeks and less than 40	40 weeks and less than 50	50 weeks and not more than 52		
Forewoman	..	2	2	3	2	11	20	40	50
Designer	25	9	13	8	10	20	14	99	23
Trimmer	45	21	24	7	6	25	8	136	11
Copyist	408	123	205	100	112	148	78	1,174	13
Maker	141	61	104	38	59	125	23	551	17
Preparer	150	71	91	35	42	24	11	424	10
Improver	29	17	32	12	20	23	4	137	14
Apprentice	97	40	58	25	13	8	6	247	9
Machine operator	33	14	28	12	8	12	25	132	17
Stock and floor girl	10	5	9	5	7	10	18	64	34
Errand girl	10	6	9	3	1	3	1	33	11
Flower or feather hand	2	1	4	3	3	14	5	32	42
Straw sewer	6	5	11	2	..	6	..	30	14
Crown sewer	6	3	2	7	4	3	5	30	26
Crimper	1	7	7	6	..	..	..	21	14
Cutter	1	1	2	3	2	1	8	18	40
Packer	1	2	1	2	1	..	5	12	30
Shopper	..	..	1	..	1	1	6	9	51
Liner	1	..	1	..	..	1	..	3	10
Frame maker	..	..	3	..	..	..	..	3	15
Hand blocker	1	1	..	..	..	..	..	2	6
Total	967	389	607	271	291	435	237	3,197[c]	14

[a] See footnote a, Table 32, p. 203.

[b] The formula used throughout the report (except in Table 32, pp. 203–4) in calculating the median was as follows: (King, W. I.: Elements of Statistical Method, p. 129.)

Let m = the median
c = the class interval of the class containing the median
k = the lower limit of the class
f = the number of items in the class
i = the number of items up from the lower limit of the class at which the median item occurs

Then

$$m = k + \frac{c(2i-1)}{2f}$$

For example, in Table 10, in computing the median for the total column,
c = 10 weeks
k = 10 weeks
f = 607
i = 243

$$m = 10 \text{ wks.} + \frac{10 \text{ wks.}\ (2 \times 243 - 1)}{2 \times 607} = 10 \text{ wks.} + \frac{4{,}850 \text{ wks.}}{1{,}214} = 14 \text{ wks.}$$

[c] Of the 3,983 women who appeared on the payroll at any time during the year, occupations were not ascertained for six, and 780 were employed a week or less and have been omitted.

All workers who appeared on the payrolls a week or less are omitted from this table. Of the 3,197 included, only 237, or 7 per cent, were on the payroll as long as fifty weeks. This proportion varied from 50 per cent for forewomen to 2 per cent for apprentices, 7 per cent for copyists, 14 per cent for designers, 28 per cent for stock girls and floor girls, 4 per cent for makers, and 3 per cent for preparers. In the ranks of experienced workers as well as among the learners frequent shifts occur.

The usual length of experience in one shop was ascertained not from the payrolls but from the cards filled by workers employed at the time of the inquiry. Table 11 shows both the period of employment in one shop and the length of experience in the trade. It is based on the answers to two questions*: "How long have you been working for this firm?" and "How long have you been in this trade or business?" The facts were not intended to show the amount of employment in a given period, but the length of experience without deductions for absences.

Of 1,359 workers in this group, as many as 422 had been in the shop less than a year and only 85 had been employed in the same establishment ten years or longer. That this record was due not to such brief experience but to shifts from one shop to another is demonstrated by comparison with the second column, showing that only 85, or 6.3

* See card D, p. 243.

TABLE 11.—YEARS EMPLOYED IN PRESENT ESTABLISHMENT AND YEARS OF EXPERIENCE IN THE TRADE, FOR WOMEN EMPLOYED IN MILLINERY ESTABLISHMENTS IN NEW YORK CITY, AS SHOWN BY CURRENT PAYROLL. 1914

Years	Women who have been specified number of years			
	In present establishment		In millinery trade	
	Number	Per cent	Number	Per cent
Less than 1 year	422	31.1	85	6.3
1 year and less than 2	227	16.7	83	6.1
2 years and less than 3	150	11.0	117	8.7
3 years and less than 4	139	10.2	144	10.7
4 years and less than 5	126	9.3	141	10.4
5 years and less than 6	65	4.8	126	9.3
6 years and less than 7	48	3.5	98	7.3
7 years and less than 8	35	2.6	94	7.0
8 years and less than 9	37	2.7	80	5.9
9 years and less than 10	25	1.8	73	5.4
10 years and less than 15	70	5.2	212	15.7
15 years and less than 20	11	.8	57	4.2
20 years or more	4	.3	41	3.0
Total	1,359[a]	100.0	1,351[a]	100.0

[a] Of the 1,363 women for whom workers' records were secured, four did not state years in present establishment and 12 did not give information as to years in the trade.

per cent, had had less than a year's experience as milliners; and while as many as 52 per cent had worked in the trade less than six years, a fairly large proportion, 23 per cent, reported a career of ten years or longer. It is clear that the working period is not very long, but that the employment in any one shop is very much shorter. Indeed, from the evidence in Table 12, the shops themselves do not appear to have long histories, although they are not so extraordinarily shortlived as was stated by one employer, who declared that the average retail shop lasted only five years.

TABLE 12.—YEARS 50 MILLINERY ESTABLISHMENTS HAD BEEN IN BUSINESS AND MAXIMUM FORCE OF WOMEN EMPLOYED. 1913

Years in business	Firms	Maximum force in 1913
Less than 1 year	2	40
1 year and less than 5	1	22
5 years and less than 10	19	616
10 years and less than 15	9	358
15 years and less than 20	7	383
20 years and less than 30	7	496
30 years and less than 40	1	57
40 years and less than 50	2	188
50 years or more	2	153
Total	50[a]	2,313[a]

[a] Seven firms of the 57 for which records were secured in the payroll study, employing a maximum force of 237 women, did not report number of years in business.

Although our enforced selection of shops in which satisfactory payroll data could be secured* tended to the choice of the better organized and

* In tabulating the facts about 149 shops investigated by us, including not only those in which payrolls were studied but others in which general inquiry was made, we found that in 103 we had secured data about the number of years of their existence. Six had been opened within a year, 20 others had a history of less than five years, 29, the largest group, between five and ten years, 19 between ten and fifteen, 22 between fifteen and twenty-five, five between twenty-five and fifty, and two for fifty years or more.

presumably more permanent establishments, only five of 50 reporting on this point had been in existence thirty years or longer. On the other hand, only three had started business within five years. In some instances employes in the older establishments could boast of long periods of service, extending even to forty years or more, but they were exceptional.

These facts all relate to the industry and the shop; and although they demonstrate the trade conditions experienced by the workers, they tell us nothing of how the workers adjust themselves to these conditions, how well they succeed in finding other work, and how much time they lose in a year. It was to secure information of this kind that we interviewed the girls themselves in their own homes.* It is not easy, however, to get the facts accurately, for the more irregular a girl's employment the more difficult it is for her to remember how much time she has lost, or even how many jobs she has had. One woman explained that she could not estimate the time lost because she went to the shop every day in the hope of getting some work. She was always paid by the piece, and the coming of slack season was heralded by a decline in her earnings as the amount of work given her grew less. "They never discharge anyone," she said. "You just stay until you are starved out."

Another reported ten positions between November, 1910, and April, 1914—seven in wholesale

* See description of methods of investigation, pp. 19–21.

millinery, two in braid manufacturing in the dull season in millinery, and one in the wholesale drug business. "There is one thing sure," said her brother admiringly, "she never stays home idle. If she is laid off one night, she starts off the next morning and doesn't come home until she has got a job." Although not all the workers are as resourceful, and not all have so varied a trade career, an accurate account of the year is almost impossible to secure from a large number of the workers. It certainly could not be obtained from payrolls in a city like New York, for even if it were possible to include all millinery shops in the study it would not give us the facts about the employment of milliners in other industries. Even for millinery alone it would be impossible, since many shops keep no payrolls and in others an attempt to identify workers in their progress from shop to shop would be fruitless. Thus, although the workers' account of themselves may often be inaccurate because of the tricks of memory, nevertheless the information cannot be obtained in any other way. As it stands, it is certainly illustrative; and the circumstances of the interviews in the homes of the workers, and the experience of the investigators in making such inquiries give confidence in the results. Table 13 shows the number of weeks of employment in millinery as reported by the 196 whose experience in that trade had extended over the period of a year or longer and who gave us a trustworthy account.

TABLE 13.—WEEKS MILLINERY WORKERS INTERVIEWED AT HOME WERE EMPLOYED IN MILLINERY DURING YEAR PREVIOUS TO INVESTIGATION

Weeks	Women
Less than 10 weeks	4
10 weeks and less than 15	3
15 weeks and less than 20	2
20 weeks and less than 25	5
25 weeks and less than 30	14
30 weeks and less than 35	19
35 weeks and less than 40	29
40 weeks and less than 45	29
45 weeks and less than 52	75
52 weeks	16
Total	196[a]

[a] Of the 234 milliners who were wage-earners during the full past year, 38 did not give a full account of their year's work.

Only 14 were employed less than twenty-five weeks, while 91 were at work in their industry forty-five weeks or longer, a fact which, if true, indicates skill in finding work since we have already seen how rare it is to be kept steadily in one shop as long as forty-five weeks. Of course, during some of these weeks the employment was only partial. On the other hand, it should be noticed that only 16 reported a full year's work in millinery, and 77 said that they were milliners from thirty to forty-five weeks, implying that for them the time out of the industry ranged from seven to twenty-two weeks. The number reporting some loss of time because of slack season was 152, because of part time employment 71, because of vacation without pay 22, holidays without pay

99, quitting job voluntarily 17, illness 35, and other causes 20. In some instances the same girl reported all these causes of loss in her year's history. Of the 189 giving a full enough account of their year's work to justify tabulation, only 24 said that they had lost no time for any cause. Table 14 shows the loss of time as the milliners reported it.

TABLE 14.—TIME OUT OF EMPLOYMENT AND TOTAL TIME FOR WHICH PAY WAS LOST, IN MILLINERY AND IN SUBSIDIARY OCCUPATIONS, DURING YEAR PREVIOUS TO INVESTIGATION, BY MILLINERY WORKERS INTERVIEWED AT HOME

Weeks	Women unemployed specified number of weeks because of		Women losing pay for specified number of weeks[a]
	Slack season	All causes	
None	46	24	4
1 week and less than 4	35	35	24
4 weeks and less than 8	44	44	41
8 weeks and less than 12	24	18	15
12 weeks and less than 16	21	28	32
16 weeks and less than 20	16	20	24
20 weeks and less than 30	12	17	20
30 weeks or more . .	..	3	3
Total	198[b]	189[b]	163[b]

[a] Includes time lost for holidays without pay, part time, vacations without pay, etc., even while worker's name was still on the payroll of the establishment. It covers all time for which full pay was not drawn, as well as time actually unemployed.

[b] Of the 234 women who were wage-earners during the full past year, 36 did not report the number of weeks unemployed because of slack season, 45 did not state the weeks unemployed from all causes, and 71 did not give information as to the total time for which pay was lost.

The table shows the actual loss of time in the year, taking account of periods filled by employment in other occupations besides millinery. Three of 189 whose records seemed full and trustworthy lost thirty weeks or more, while the largest group, 44, lost from four to eight weeks. The total loss reported by this group of 189 was 1,704 weeks, or an average of nine weeks for each worker out of the possible 52 of a full working year. That is to say, these workers lost 17 per cent of their normal working period, even though some of them found work in other occupations when the season was dull in millinery.

Had no effort been made to find other positions, the loss of time would doubtless have been greater. Of 223 reporting the number of changes in jobs during the year, only 117 had made no change, 30 had changed once, 31 twice, 21 three times, 15 four times, and nine five times or more. Sometimes it was a change from one position to another in millinery, for 183 said that they had worked in but one industry during the year. Thirty-six reported two different occupations, seven reported three, and two reported four or five, the remaining six of the 234 at work a year or more in the trade making no report on this point.

Table 15 shows the extent to which the women interviewed had had experience in different branches of the trade.

A large group, 104, have had experience in both retail and wholesale shops, while 76 have worked in retail only and 66 have limited their experience to wholesale. The description of processes of work has shown how different are the demands in some of the wholesale workrooms compared with the demands of some retail shops. In many of the wholesale factories wages are paid by the piece and speed is essential. In the best type of retail

TABLE 15.—EXPERIENCE IN DIFFERENT BRANCHES OF THE TRADE FOR MILLINERY WORKERS INTERVIEWED AT HOME

Branch of trade	Women who have worked in each specified branch of trade
Retail only	76
Wholesale only	66
Retail and wholesale	104
Total	246[a]

[a] Of the 252 women interviewed at home, six did not state the branch of the trade in which they had worked.

production the quality of the work must be of the finest, and experience as a piece worker in wholesale would be a positive handicap rather than an advantage. Moreover, the overlapping of the seasons makes employers averse to employing girls from another branch of the trade, who may leave them to return to their own specialty before the season is completed. "I cannot go back to the wholesale shop where I worked last season," said one milliner; "if you work in wholesale in the off-retail season, you have to work in a different place each season, because they don't want to take girls who won't stay."

Frequent changes are obviously characteristic of the trade careers of milliners, but these are not due wholly to the direct effects of short seasons. The indirect effect is undoubtedly to produce a certain restlessness which accounts, in part, for the irresponsible attitude of which employers complain. Moreover, to change positions is part of the reasoned practice of some of the workers, who say that only by going from shop to shop can you really advance. "If you stay too long in a place," said one girl, "you begin to think more of the shop than you do of yourself, and they will let you stay at wages lower than they know you could get somewhere else."

The suggestion is often made that unemployment due to seasonal fluctuations may be eliminated or, at least, decreased by a process of dovetailing occupations whose busy seasons occur at different times of the year. In the Manhattan Trade School for Girls in New York, milliners are taught lampshade making as a subsidiary trade in which they may work in dull season, especially before Christmas. For a limited group this is certainly feasible, especially as lampshade making and hat trimming have much in common in essential processes. The industry is so much smaller than millinery, however, that it could never offer opportunities to more than a small proportion of milliners. The records of the girls whom we interviewed seemed to show that no single occupation had been demonstrated to be peculiarly suitable as a resource for them. Table 16 shows the occupations in which they have worked.

TABLE 16.—SUBSIDIARY WORK IN WHICH 79 MILLINERY WORKERS INTERVIEWED AT HOME HAVE BEEN EMPLOYED SINCE ENTERING THE MILLINERY TRADE

Kind of work	Positions held
Manufacturing	
Clothing	29
Textiles and miscellaneous sewed materials	20
Paper goods	8
Artificial flowers and feathers	6
Headwear (other than millinery)	6
Rubber, fur, and leather goods	6
Miscellaneous manufactured goods	5
Foodstuffs and tobacco	4
Home work (beading)	1
Work in stores	19
Office work	12
Domestic service	2
Teaching	1
Total	119[a]

[a] These 119 positions were held by only 79 women. Of the 252 women interviewed at home, 173 have done no subsidiary work since entering the millinery trade.

Of the 252 women interviewed in their homes, 173 reported no occupation other than millinery. Among the remaining 79 were distributed the 119 positions listed in the table. Some of the workers obviously had tried several different trades. The largest group of positions was in some branch of the clothing industry, and the second largest group was in textile manufacture or sewing on miscellaneous articles. Saleswork was third in the list. Sometimes girls employed in millinery workrooms in department stores may be transferred to the counters during the Christmas sales which follow the millinery season. An employer in one of the largest retail millinery establishments said that he regularly sent his workers to three department stores for holiday work, which carried them over the dull season in millinery. In establishments having also a dressmaking department, milliners are sometimes transferred to it. Upholstery was named by several girls as a possible subsidiary occupation in which the milliner's skill with the needle was useful. Neckwear making, or sewing on fancy articles of various kinds, was sometimes found to be a part of the work of a millinery shop, making it possible to retain the workers longer. In a wholesale shop the girls at one table had worked out a plan whereby they took turns in coming to work in dull season, two appearing one day, and two others the next. They divided their earnings at the end of the week, having saved time and carfare by this co-operative arrangement.

One girl, who had been at work six years, gave us a list of the occupations in which she had worked in dull season. They included the making of handkerchiefs, paper boxes, ladies' waists, babies' hats, and buttonholes in sweaters, stock work in a leather goods factory, canvassing for a music school, taking charge of her brothers' cleaning and dyeing store, selling hats in a millinery shop on the lower East Side, saleswork in a dry-goods store, and the manufacture of embroidery. She reported also seven different jobs in millinery, which were all that she could remember. "Between seasons I take anything," said a girl who had been addressing envelopes for a mail order house. "The work doesn't pay much, but it's better than nothing."

Illustrations could be multiplied to show the many different combinations of occupations secured by these girls. The one common element seems to be the chance method of selection. "We take any kind of work that's advertised," said one. Advertisements in the daily papers are, indeed, the chief means of organizing the labor market in the millinery trade, and it is, of course, a very wasteful method. With the development of public employment bureaus, it is possible that milliners may secure more effective information about openings in their own industry or in other occupations. At present the nearest approach to an employment exchange in the trade is the activity of some wholesale houses which not only supply their customers with millinery materials, but also secure milliners for them, especially those who come from out of town. One forewoman, who takes a great interest in finding good positions for her girls, and frequently recommends them for work in other cities and towns, boasted that in every state in the Union one could find milliners who had once worked under her direction in New York. In another establishment we were told that because of the reputation of the firm they have many more applicants for work than they can engage. They keep a card file of all former employes, and when their out-of-town customers need trimmers they recommend those whose references prove satisfactory. This is, of course, a convenience to customers and an advantage to the girls, who sometimes find in that way an opportunity to gain valuable experience.

In reading the statistics of irregular employment which have been outlined in this chapter, it should be kept in mind that one of the characteristics of irregularity is its own variation from year to year. The duration of the season, the proportion of workers retained in the dull months, and even the influences which produce irregularity, all change from year to year. Changes in style result in rearrangement in the proportion of different groups of workers employed. When net or lace hats are worn, which require fine hand-work, makers will have a good season, and inexperienced girls may have greater difficulty in entering the trade. When the demand is for machine-made hats with very little trimming, machine operators will be employed in larger numbers and girls who can sew on a bow or adjust a buckle will find their opportunity. If the weather is bad in the spring, buying is less brisk, and orders are less plentiful. One firm, at least, lost money in 1913 because of floods in the spring in the Middle West, in the territory where it had developed its best market. Above the necessary minimum spent in buying hats for mere head protection is a wide margin of expenditure for luxury within which the variations may be very great. It is within this margin that weather, the attractiveness of the style, and the state of the money market exert their influence. "I have been in this trade for thirty-five years," said one employer, "and I tell you it is a treacherous business. You never can tell what is going to happen. Take this season: I had figured on fur hats and suddenly in December wool hats come in. I lost a thousand dollars in December. The trade is changed; there are machine hats now, and if hand-made hats don't sell, we don't need any milliners."

It must be admitted that to prolong the seasons or to regularize employment would not be an easy task, and it was probably not to be expected that in our interviews with employers we would find evidence of organized effort to remedy the condition. Most of them would agree with the milliner who said that the trade will always be seasonal. "Everybody wants hats at once," she said, "and there are so many girls that employers can get them for as short a time as they need them. In every trade," she added, "there are too many workers."

Occasionally, however, hints were given which

suggest the possibility of improvement. "My seasons are long because I work on orders," said the owner of a small but select retail shop. "I don't do as they do on the Avenue. There they make hundreds of hats at the beginning of the season and then lay off the girls. Last season F——— (naming a large establishment) laid off his girls six weeks before I thought of doing it." It seems probable that she was right and that she was indicating one cause of irregularity. It is possible, and it seems to be the practice, to make up a large part of the stock at the beginning of the season and then retain only enough girls in the workroom to make the alterations required for individual customers. It should be understood that this is different from what is ordinarily known as making up stock in advance, a practice which might make it possible to spread the work over the dull season. The custom to which reference has just been made implies rather a rush of work after the fashions for the season are known, but in advance of individual orders. We were told by a number of employers that it was possible formerly to foretell more or less accurately what styles would be in demand, and to make the hats in advance of the season, but that now the fashion varies so much from season to season that work cannot begin until the decrees of fashion are pronounced.

One shop now adopts the policy of engaging fewer workers in busy season so that the period of their employment may be prolonged. A wholesale establishment makes a practice of offering special attractions between seasons at little or no profit in order to keep its workroom open. The employer pointed out that few firms know how to make or to sell these specialties. For the most part the concentration of orders in a few months of the year is accepted as inevitable, and the only deliberate policy adopted by any large number of firms with reference to the workers is to lay off first those who have been engaged last, thus giving the advantage to the girls who have worked the longest for them. Not even this custom is universal, however. Some employers told us frankly that the payroll determined their practice and that the highest paid were the first to be laid off.

As to whether the tendency is toward longer or shorter seasons, opinions were divided. One woman who had worked in the trade in New York for nearly thirty years declared that until a few years ago she kept busy in the shop almost all the year, but that now it was necessary for her to take another position, sewing for an interior decorator in the slack season, which was much longer than formerly. Another, with twelve years' experience, thought the busy seasons shorter than they used to be, although wages, especially for learners, were higher. In a wholesale shop we were told that seasons were longer than they used to be, because women now buy mid-season hats and tire of them more quickly than they did years ago. In the winter of 1916–17, one Fifth Avenue house was reported to be engaging workers under contract for fifty-two weeks. This surprising development was explained as due in part to a scarcity of experienced workers, caused by the abnormal industrial prosperity then existing. A retail dealer said that, hereafter, she would keep her shop open in August, instead of closing it as had been her custom, because the new fashion of wearing velvet hats in August and straw hats in January was creating a demand for mid-season work. It was interesting that the women who had worked in the trade in England were unanimous in their testimony that no such violent fluctuations disturbed the regularity of employment there, and that although extra hands were sometimes taken on in a busy week, the regular force had more steady work than in the United States.

Doubtless the differences of opinion as to conditions here were due in large part to differences in individual experience. We have no data to enable us to trace tendencies with any degree of confidence in the conclusions. It is clear, however, that some firms succeed very much better than others in prolonging the seasons. On this point a comparison between five establishments, which are generally regarded as leaders in the trade in New York, is illuminating. Table 17 brings out marked differences between them.

Of the total number of workers employed at any time during the year, D kept the largest propor-

TABLE 17.—DURATION OF EMPLOYMENT OF WOMEN IN FIVE LEADING MILLINERY ESTABLISHMENTS IN NEW YORK CITY, FOR THE CALENDAR YEAR 1913[a]

Firm	Maximum force in each establishment	Number of weeks in which force exceeded the average	Women employed in each establishment					Per cent of women on payroll 26 weeks or more	Per cent on payroll 6 weeks or more who were kept 26 weeks or more
			1 week or less	Over 1 week and less than 6	6 weeks and less than 26	26 weeks or more	Total		
A	131	31	1	8	51	98	158	62	66
B	53	24	24	16	42	24	106	23	36
C	84	33	15	22	31	60	128	47	66
D	69	34	1	7	18	58	84	69	76
E	57	30	11	7	21	44	83	53	68

[a] Of the five establishments, two were in the retail branch of the trade and three in the retail-wholesale branch.

tion on the payroll twenty-six weeks or longer—69 per cent as compared with 23 per cent kept by B. D also showed a greater number of weeks in which the force exceeded the average—thirty-four weeks out of the fifty-two as compared with B again, where the force was only twenty-four weeks within this limit, while the other three showed approximately the same length for their busy season between D and B. The duration of the rush season, therefore, does vary in shops of the same grade and branch of the trade. Further evidence also of change in the personnel of the force in these prominent establishments is given in the percentage of the workers on the payroll six weeks or more who were kept for half the year or longer. The percentages here vary from 36 to 76, again with B at the bottom and D at the top.

Tendencies vary from shop to shop, but assuredly it is clear that the trade is characterized by extreme irregularity of employment, due chiefly to irregularity of demand, and that at present no forces are evident which are powerful enough to effect a change.

CHAPTER V

WAGES AND WORK CONDITIONS

AN UNUSUALLY fortunate milliner, whose record we had copied from the payroll, had had the good luck to be employed fifty-one weeks in twelve months in the same shop. In the beginning of the year she was paid at the rate of $13 a week, in the thirty-second week her wages were increased to $14, yet her annual earnings from that shop were only $580 instead of $697 which would have been her income had she been employed the full fifty-two weeks at the rate of $13 for thirty-one weeks and $14 for twenty-one weeks. The difference was due chiefly to the fact that in the dull season, at the beginning and the end and the middle of the year, seventeen weeks in all, her pay was reduced to $8.00 in consideration of steady employment. Had this reduction been due to employment for fewer hours in the day, it would have seemed to her a fair arrangement, but to be required to work full time for little more than half her usual wages was an injustice of which she complained vigorously.

A Russian Jewish girl had also a record of fifty-one weeks of employment, with a wage rate of $8.00 for eighteen weeks, $7.00 for an eight-weeks' period when work was slack, $8.00 for four weeks, and $9.00 for the last twenty-one weeks. Her income for the year was $392. Her regular rate of $8.00, with the increase later to $9.00, would have amounted to an annual wage of $437. Even allowing for the slack season reduction, she might have expected $429. But she was laid off for one week without pay, and during eleven weeks she worked less than six days, receiving correspondingly less wages. Three weeks in the spring and two weeks in the autumn she worked overtime, earning in all $8.33 more than her usual wages, a sum which is, of course, included in her actual yearly income. Nevertheless, her loss in the year amounted to $45, the difference between the annual rate of $437 and her actual earnings of $392—a loss equal to more than 10 per cent of what might be considered her normal income.

Another girl, a piece worker employed fifty weeks, had found that the contents of her pay envelopes varied from $2.51 to $18.58 a week, with an average of $9.36. She earned $468 in the year. The fluctuations for her took the form of smaller quantities of work rather than reduced weekly rates. It was necessary to go regularly to the factory, however, to be on hand for unexpected orders, even though she might earn only $2.51 in a week. All these experiences demonstrate the difficulty of interpreting wage rates in a seasonal industry in terms of actual income, and the necessity for keeping in mind the facts about irregularity of employment in discussing information about the wage scale. To determine income, it is necessary to know not only the wage rates but the actual earnings after deductions are made for weeks out of work, for loss of time in a working week, for fines or other causes, taking into consideration also any extra earnings for overtime, or any bonuses received. The wage statistics which we have secured have a peculiar value because in them an exact allowance has been made for all these factors.

It will be recalled that we obtained four different kinds of wage data.* First, we copied the total wages paid and the number of women employed in millinery work in each establishment each week in the year. These facts have already been presented. They show fluctuations in employment but they do not reveal individual earnings. Second, we copied from the current payroll the wage rates and the actual earnings of every worker then employed, and correlated these facts with information obtained from the worker's own written answers to questions regarding age, nationality, length of time employed in the shop and in the trade, and whether boarding or living at home. Third, we copied the wage rates and the actual earnings during the entire period of employment in the year in a single establishment for every worker appearing on the payrolls of the shops investigated at any time in the fifty-two weeks between January 1st and December 31st, 1913. By divid-

* See description of methods of investigation, pp. 8–10, 19–21.

In a Retail Shop

ing the sum of the total earnings of each worker during the period of her employment by the number of weeks worked, we determined the average weekly wage in which allowance is made for all additions and deductions occurring within the working period. In this set of figures no account was taken of the weeks in which no wages were received, since we could not be sure that the time may not have been spent at work in another shop, and unless we had known the earnings elsewhere it would not have been fair to estimate the total income. Fourth, we interviewed a group of 252 girls at home, and secured from them as accurate as possible an account of their whole trade career, especially the regularity of their employment and income during the preceding year. Some of these girls had worked in shops in which we had copied the payrolls, so that we had documentary evidence of their earnings in one position. In many cases, for reasons already explained in discussing the difficulty of determining loss of time in the year, the data secured in these interviews can be regarded as only approximately accurate. Combined with the other statistics presented, however, the information is certainly of value in throwing light on wage facts which cannot be secured from payrolls. The various series of statistics will be presented in the order in which they have been outlined, beginning with the second, since the first have already been discussed in the preceding chapter.

FACTS FROM THE CURRENT PAYROLL

It should be explained first that the two methods of payment prevailing in millinery, as in many other trades, are designated as week work and piece work. As the terms imply, the girls who work by the week receive a fixed rate regardless of the exact number of hats on which they have worked, while piece workers' earnings depend on the number of hats, or parts of hats, completed. Retail shops always pay by the week, while in wholesale the practice varies. Obviously, the piece-work system would apply only to orders for several hats of the same kind. Given that condition, however, it is a matter of choice on the part of the firm as to whether wages will be figured by the week or the piece. Some wholesale shops have both week and piece workers. "We pay by the piece," said one employer. "The girls like it better and we like it better. With week work, the girls have their eyes on the clock all the time waiting for six o'clock, but with piece work they are trying to see how much money they can make."

Curiously enough, we found no instance of piece work in the wholesale shops on Division Street, an instance apparently of the strength of a trade custom in a community, for Division Street is a community in the industry. One employer there referred to the prevalence of piece work in the Broadway wholesale houses and expressed the opinion that in time the system might reach

Division Street. He thought that it was an advantage from the employer's point of view, since he can estimate costs better. Before setting the price, he estimates the girls' capacity, and he makes the rate as low as he can, he said. He thought the girls had more advantage in week work. Division Street employers, however, do not forego entirely the benefits of piece work, for as one girl explained: "They pay by the week but they count the hats twice a day, and if you don't finish as many as they want, they scold you. They would like you to turn out 10 or 15 a day." An employer on Broadway declared that the piece-work system encouraged "botchy work" and she preferred week workers, but, she added, "my week workers have to make their wages by turning out so many hats a week." Other employers complained that piece workers are much less regular in attendance than week workers, since when they are paid by the piece they feel free to come later in the morning. They are "on their own time," as they express it. Piece work is of greatest advantage when speed is more important than quality. "I am a very quick worker, but a very poor milliner," said one honest girl.

In the various shops visited 1,951 were recorded on the payroll at the date of the investigation, and of these, 1,363 working in the shops at the time of the visits filled out personal records.* The median

* Detailed tables showing both rates and earnings will be found in the Supplementary Report, Tables 33–41, p. 205 ff

rate of pay for week workers as shown on the pay-rolls was $10.77, half the workers being rated at less than this amount and half above it. Rates in retail were higher than in wholesale. The median actual earnings of both week workers and piece workers amounted to $9.69. It is a notable characteristic of millinery that the range of wages is wide, varying from 50 cents to $150 a week, with 15 in every hundred earning $15 or more. The proportion of women earning $15 or more in all trades in New York state, according to the census of 1905,* was only 1.8 per cent, and the percentage earning less than $8.00 was 73, so that apparently millinery is not one of the low-paid industries for women. Of the occupations investigated by the Factory Investigating Commission, millinery had the highest wage scale, as Table 18 shows.

Of the milliners, 53 per cent earned less than $10 as compared with 70 per cent of the women in department stores, 85.5 per cent of the paper box makers, and 93 per cent of the candy makers. On the other hand, none of these other industries had quite so large a group earning less than $3.00 a week. Before paying any compliments to employers in the millinery trade because of the showing in this table, it should be remembered that none of these industries had such violent fluctuations in employment as were found in millinery shops.

* United States Census of Manufactures, 1905. Bulletin 93, Earnings of Wage-Earners, p. 151.

TABLE 18.—ACTUAL WEEKLY EARNINGS OF WOMEN EMPLOYED IN MILLINERY ESTABLISHMENTS, DEPARTMENT STORES, PAPER BOX FACTORIES, AND CANDY FACTORIES IN NEW YORK CITY, 1913, COMPARED BY CUMULATIVE PERCENTAGES[a]

Weekly earnings	Per cent of women earning less than the specified amounts employed in			
	Millinery shops	Department stores[b]	Paper box factories[b]	Candy factories[b]
Less than $3	5.9	1.4	2.8	5.3
Less than $4	9.6	6.8	8.8	12.3
Less than $5	14.4	17.7	21.0	30.1
Less than $6	20.6	25.3	38.1	54.5
Less than $7	26.9	36.3	52.3	70.2
Less than $8	34.7	49.2	64.2	80.6
Less than $9	44.1	61.5	75.4	87.9
Less than $10	52.7	70.1	85.5	92.8
Less than $12	67.3	81.3	95.5	97.9
Less than $15	84.8	91.0	99.5	99.4
Less than $18	91.2	95.6	99.95	99.7
Less than $20	92.6	97.0	99.97	99.8
Less than $25	95.0	98.6	100.0	99.9
Less than $30	96.7	99.3	..	100.0
Less than $35	97.6	99.6	..	..
Less than $40	98.4	99.8	..	..
$40 or more	1.6	.2	..	..
Median earnings[c]	$9.69	$8.07	$6.83	$5.79

[a] New York State Factory Investigating Commission. Fourth Report, 1915. Vol. II, p. 384, and Vol. III, pp. 992, 1075, 1081.

[b] The percentages for department stores cover only the stock and sales force, and for the paper box and candy establishments only the factory workers. The office force, shipping and delivery departments, etc., have not been included, since they were not covered for millinery shops, and their inclusion in the figures for the other three industries would invalidate the comparison with millinery.

[c] See footnote b, p. 83.

Variation in wages according to length of experience is probably a more or less accurate indication of whether or not skill is required. In occupations requiring little skill, those in which experience counts less than some other factors, like speed, endurance, or muscular development, we do not expect to find marked differences in earning power related to differences in the length of employment. Millinery, however, is a skilled occupation, requiring speed in some of its branches and delicacy of touch in others, but always demanding practice for successful work. Table 19 shows the median rates and earnings according to length of experience.

The median rates of wages show a steady progression from $4.09 for those employed less than one year, to $22.50 for those who have had from fifteen to twenty years' experience. Then the median rate drops, but the numbers in the groups having had an experience of twenty years and longer are too small for definite conclusions. The actual earnings of the week workers are generally less than the rates of pay. Among piece workers the range of median earnings was not so wide as for week workers, possibly an indication that as speed is the essential requirement in piece work, length of experience counts less than among week workers where skill of a more delicate type, developed by a long period of training, is the chief consideration. It is also true that piece workers in wholesale shops are usually copyists and hence do not represent any variety of occupations, whereas the week workers include all occupations

TABLE 19.—MEDIAN WEEKLY RATES OF WAGES AND EARNINGS, BY YEARS IN THE TRADE, FOR WOMEN EMPLOYED IN MILLINERY, AS SHOWN BY CURRENT PAYROLL. 1914

Years in the trade	Women reporting weekly rate of wages		Women reporting actual weekly earnings			
			Number		Median earnings[a]	
	Number	Median rate	Week workers	Piece workers	Week workers	Piece workers
Less than 1 year	85	$4.09	85	..	$3.91	..
1 year and less than 2	63	6.04	63	9	5.77	$4.50
2 years and less than 3	88	7.05	88	21	6.55	8.17
3 years and less than 5	213	8.99	213	49	8.65	8.79
5 years and less than 7	166	11.54	166	41	11.14	10.39
7 years and less than 10	186	13.13	186	49	12.70	9.06
10 years and less than 15	159	15.24	159	44	14.81	9.57
15 years and less than 20	41	22.50	41	15	22.50	11.25
20 years or more	25	17.50	25	16	17.00	9.00
Total	1,026	$10.82	1,026	244	$10.33	$9.21

[a] See footnote b, p. 83.

from an apprentice to a designer, and it is natural that their pay should advance as through experience they become more capable of the more highly skilled processes. The copyist who is a piece worker could not advance further, even after years of experience, unless she shifted to week work as a trimmer or designer.

Age is, of course, a factor in wages. Median rates were found to vary from $4.14 for workers under sixteen to $20 for those of forty-five or older. In actual earnings for the entire group the range was not so wide, as the median for girls under sixteen was $4.00, and for women between thirty-five and forty who earned the maximum, $15. Of the 125 receiving rates of less than $6.00, 83 were under eighteen and 42 were eighteen or older. Of the 180 women of thirty years or older as many as 113 received less than $16. The higher wages are not attained by more than a small proportion of the workers and then only for the more mature.

It was for forewomen and designers that the prizes were chiefly reserved. The median rate for designers was $37,* for forewomen $24.50, while for apprentices it was $3.50. For trimmers the median wage received was $14, copyists $13, makers $12.50, preparers $8.50, and improvers $6.00.

A tabulation of earnings according to nativity seemed worth making. This showed a median wage of $9.94 for the foreign born, $10.08 for the native born, and $10.02 for the two groups com-

* Exact medians are given in Table 39, p. 215.

bined.* The differences are too slight to be significant. Or, perhaps, on the contrary, it is very significant that the foreign workers are not seriously underbidding the native in millinery shops. As might be expected from the fact that the foreign born predominate only in wholesale, their occupations are largely those of the wholesale trade, chiefly the work of copyists. Of the 31 forewomen in the group giving information as to nativity, only seven were foreign born; and of the 44 designers who reported on this point, 25 were born in the United States.

FACTS FROM THE ANNUAL PAYROLL

The facts which have been given so far in this chapter all relate to the current payroll in each establishment; that is, to a single week. Information from the annual payroll will carry us further toward an estimate of the income of milliners. It will not, however, take us the whole distance. Although the agents of the Factory Investigating Commission were sanguine enough to use as a heading for the card on which to transcribe earnings the caption "Individual Annual Earnings," it is already evident from the discussion, especially in the preceding chapter, that no such assumption

* In the group of 226 girls interviewed by us who gave information as to nativity and wages, the median wage for the 119 foreign born was $10.37, for the 18 native born of native parentage, $6.75, and for the 89 native born of foreign parentage, $8.50. Of course, the numbers are too few and the factors entering into wage determinations too complex, to draw any conclusion from the data except that there is no evidence of underbidding on the part of foreigners.

can be justified. Unless a worker appeared on the payroll 52 times in the year, we cannot be sure that in periods of unemployment in one shop she may not have been at work in another, either in millinery or in any other industry, and the payroll which we happen to be studying will not reveal her total income. Even if we find that she was employed throughout the year, we do not know how much she may have earned by making hats at home for her own customers, or even by working in another establishment in the evening. What the payroll does show is the wage received by every employe in these shops each week in the course of a year. This is not annual income, but additional evidence regarding weekly earnings, of somewhat greater value than one week's statistics because the data extend over a longer period, thus tending to eliminate the accidents of exceptional weeks. In presenting the statistics we have not selected one typical week, but we have ascertained the total earnings of each worker and then divided this sum by the number of times her name was on the payroll, thus determining the average contents of her weekly pay envelope. If in any week her name was not on the payroll, that week was not counted in the period of employment, since its inclusion would have been based on the assumption that we could state her income throughout that period. All that we could justifiably assume was that the data showed the average contents of the pay envelopes for individual workers rather than for the group, and for the total period of employment rather than for a selected week. Table 20 shows the distribution of workers according to average weekly earnings. It excludes those who were on the payroll a week or less, presumably on trial, which did not prove satisfactory.

TABLE 20.—AVERAGE WEEKLY EARNINGS DURING PERIOD OF EMPLOYMENT FOR WOMEN EMPLOYED IN ANY ONE MILLINERY ESTABLISHMENT FOR MORE THAN ONE WEEK DURING THE CALENDAR YEAR 1913

Average weekly earnings	Women	
	Number	Per cent
Less than $2	81	2.5
$2 and less than $3	153	4.8
$3 and less than $4	168	5.2
$4 and less than $5	244	7.6
$5 and less than $6	284	8.9
$6 and less than $7	319	10.0
$7 and less than $8	284	8.9
$8 and less than $9	271	8.5
$9 and less than $10	293	9.1
$10 and less than $12	482	15.0
$12 and less than $14	248	7.7
$14 and less than $16	131	4.1
$16 and less than $18	45	1.4
$18 and less than $20	53	1.7
$20 and less than $25	51	1.6
$25 and less than $30	26	.8
$30 and less than $35	20	.6
$35 and less than $40	18	.6
$40 or more	32	1.0
Total	3,203[a]	100.0

[a] Of the 3,983 women who appeared on the annual payroll at any time during the year, 780 were on the payroll a week or less in the calendar year and were omitted from this table.

It should be remembered that this table includes all the employes who stayed longer than a week in these shops in the year. We have already explained how much this number was in excess of the force required at any one time. This means that if changes occur more frequently in any one wage group, the numbers in that wage group will have greater weight in the table than their proportion in the shop at any one time would warrant. Nevertheless, these were all millinery workers in New York in the year 1913, and the table is of value in showing the average weekly earnings of each of them in one shop. The median was between $8.00 and $9.00. One in five received less than $5.00, and more than half less than $9.00. The number earning $16 or more, including all designers and forewomen, was only 245, or 7.7 per cent. As many as 7 per cent received less than $3.00. A comparison of the average earnings during the period of employment with the rates and earnings in a single week shows that for the group as a whole the median of the average earnings was $8.25 as compared with median earnings of $9.69 in a single week, and median wage rates of $10.77. These figures show the difference between a wage rate and the average contents of a pay envelope, a difference amounting in this case to $2.52, which may roughly be considered the average milliner's loss due to scattered losses of time during the period of her employment. It excludes the loss due to entire unemployment.

Some of the differences between the wage rate and actual earnings are due to deductions for such purposes as fines, which are a punitive measure to compel promptness. They are not universal, however. In one large retail establishment, for example, in which the workroom is very carefully organized and the supervising member of the firm a strict disciplinarian, no fine is ever exacted; if a girl is tardy she is reprimanded, and if it happens too often she is dismissed. This is a much more reasonable procedure than the fining system, which seems too often like a scheme of petty taxation of pay envelopes for the benefit of the firm. In one wholesale establishment which a milliner had described to us as "a place where you never get your full salary," our investigators found it almost the universal rule to dock every worker for tardiness, so that the earnings were almost invariably a few cents, at least, below the wage rate. Deductions for holidays have already been discussed.

The proportion earning the lower wages was greater among those whose terms of employment in the period studied were brief. The median wage for those at work longer than a week but less than ten weeks was $6.52; for those employed between ten and twenty weeks, $8.57; and for those at work twenty weeks or longer, $9.90. It is illuminating also to consider the proportion in the different wage groups whose records on the payroll were brief. Of the whole group, 42 per cent were on the payrolls less than ten weeks in the year. Classified according to wages, the proportion was 66 per cent of those getting less than $5.00, 45 per cent for those getting between $5.00 and $10, 25 per cent between $10 and $16, and 22 per cent for those receiving $16 or more. Apparently the greatest instability is found in the lower wage groups, a fact of importance in an effort to increase the earnings of the lowest paid workers. A short term of employment and low wages combine to reduce total receipts from a single establishment in a year to a very low level.

In 708 positions the amount received during the period of employment was less than $25, and every occupation except that of forewoman was represented in this group. The median was $99; that is, half the workers received less than that amount from one place of employment in the year for which we secured records. Of 99 designers, 44 received less than $500. The median earnings for apprentices from one shop in the year actually were as low as $22, and in no occupational group did the median exceed $250 excepting designers, for whom the median was $633, and forewomen, for whom it was $829. We have already noted the fact that forewomen are more steadily employed than other workers, and although the rate of their earnings is lower than for designers, their actual income appears to be higher.

Practically all the jobs yielding an income of less than $50 lasted less than twenty weeks in the calendar year, while all those in the groups above $800 lasted twenty weeks or longer. Actually, however, this is only another way of saying that the longer your work lasts the more you earn. The really significant fact in the table is that for the 1,235 who were on the payroll twenty weeks or longer, the median income was but $388, and only 381, or 31 per cent, received $500 or more while in one shop. Apparently a living wage for the majority of milliners is secured, if at all, only by holding more than one position in a year.

WAGES AS REPORTED BY THE WORKERS

It was necessary to talk with the girls themselves to find out how successful they were in securing more than one position in a year, and to learn as accurately as possible their total income from all the positions which they may have held. We talked with many of them also about the cost of living and asked them their opinion of the minimum wages required by milliners to maintain a healthful standard. Before presenting the facts about their wages, it may be well to describe the group, as to age, length of experience in the trade, and duration of employment in one shop, in order to compare them in these respects with the larger number investigated in the shops. The median age for the group interviewed at home was twenty years and eleven months, as compared with twenty-two years and seven months for the group of whom records were obtained in the shops. In length of experience, also, the girls in the shops had some advantage over those whom we visited at home, but in earning capacity as measured in weekly wages as well as in positions held, the latter were thoroughly representative.* It seems fair, therefore, to regard the facts about their annual earnings as indicating the income of millinery workers in general. Table 21 shows the annual income from all work, including both millinery and other occupations during the year.

The group for whom we were able to estimate the annual income numbered 176. The median weekly wage for them was $9.84. Had they been steadily employed, this would have amounted to annual earnings of $512. As a matter of fact, their actual median annual income was only $365. This discrepancy of $147, or 29 per cent of the annual rate, tells the story of irregular and seasonal employment in the millinery trade. The courageous girl who said, "I think maybe $8.00 is a large enough wage for a girl to live on if she gets it every week, but for a milliner it must be $12," was statistically accurate in her estimate of the tax which conditions in her trade levied on the possible income of the average worker. For girls earning $4.00 or less a week in millinery the median annual income was $100; for those between $4.00 and $8.00, annual earnings of $242; with $378 for workers earning between $8.00 and $12, and $506 for those earning $12 to $25 or more.

* See data in Supplementary Report, pp. 225–227.

TABLE 21.—INCOMES IN PAST YEAR, BY WEEKLY WAGES IN PRESENT OR LAST POSITION, FOR MILLINERY WORKERS INTERVIEWED AT HOME

Income in past year	Women whose weekly wages were												All women
	Less than $3	$3 and less than $4	$4 and less than $5	$5 and less than $6	$6 and less than $7	$7 and less than $8	$8 and less than $9	$9 and less than $10	$10 and less than $12	$12 and less than $15	$15 and less than $25	$25 or more	
Less than $100	1	3	..	3	..	..	..	..	..	..	..	..	7
$100 and less than $200	2	2	6	2	3	..	1	..	..	1	..	..	17
$200 and less than $300	..	..	3	4	11	7	3	4	3	1	..	..	36
$300 and less than $400	..	..	..	1	3	4	7	8	14	6	..	..	43
$400 and less than $500	..	..	..	..	..	..	4	5	10	17	..	..	36
$500 and less than $600	..	..	..	..	..	1	..	2	6	15	1	..	25
$600 and less than $800	..	..	..	..	1	..	..	..	..	4	..	..	5
$800 and less than $1,000	..	..	..	..	..	..	..	..	..	..	1	1	2
$1,000 and less than $1,500	..	..	..	..	..	..	..	..	..	..	..	1	1
$1,500 and less than $2,000	..	..	..	..	..	..	..	..	..	..	..	2	2
$2,000 or more	..	..	..	..	..	..	..	..	..	..	..	2	2
Total	3	5	9	10	18	12	15	19	33	44	2	6	176[a]
Median income[b]	$100		$242				$378			$506			$365

[a] Of the 252 women interviewed at home, 18 had not been wage-earners during the full past year, one did not give information as to weekly wage, 53 did not state yearly income, and four did not give information on either point.

[b] See footnote b, p. 83.

None had less than twenty weeks of employment. The median duration of work for the 189 girls who reported it was forty-four weeks, or about 85 per cent of the year. Of course, losses occurred within these forty-four weeks, especially for piece workers, whose earnings are lower in slack season. One girl who happened to be on the payroll the median number of weeks, forty-four in the year, having been laid off five weeks in the spring and three in the autumn, received a wage of $12 in busy season and $8.00 in dull weeks, with a total of $478 for the year. Another, on the payroll fifty-one weeks, had a nominal weekly wage of $8.00 but annual earnings of only $376, with a weekly average of $7.37 for the weeks worked, and $7.23 for the whole year. In spite of the duration of her employment in one shop, she received $32 less than the weekly rate should have brought her. Indeed, for the group who worked fifty weeks or longer, the median annual income was only $465.

In many instances the year's history included more than one position. As we have already pointed out in the preceding chapter, it was necessary in some instances to work in some other occupation besides millinery. Indeed, at the time of the interview, only 183 of the group of 252 interviewed were in millinery shops, 17 being in other occupations, and the remaining 52 out of work.

If we look over the tables in which wages are presented, we see how wide is the difference between the median wage rate of $10.77 disclosed in the current payroll (Table 33, p. 206), and the median annual income of $365 from all occupations during twelve months, ascertained in interviews with a group of girls whose weekly earning power was typical of the larger number recorded on the payrolls. With each new set of statistics the estimate was revised and reduced as new facts regarding irregular employment entered into the calculation. The weekly wage rate of $10.77 (Table 33) for week workers is larger than the earnings of $9.69 (Table 34, p. 207) for all workers in a single week. When the entire period of employment in one shop was considered and the weekly wages averaged for each worker, the median became $8.25 (Table 42, p. 220). Our study of the year's history of the girls interviewed at home showed a median annual income of $365. Aside from its significance for the millinery industry, the whole process is an interesting illustration of the characteristic dangers in handling wage data. Irregular employment from many diverse causes is a complicating factor of great importance. In the millinery industry, the data show a situation fully deserving consideration by a state commission.

STANDARDS OF LIVING

Is $365 an adequate annual income? It was not possible in this investigation to make a budget study. Moreover, we were less interested in discovering the exact expenditures of low-wage girls than in learning what standards they themselves thought necessary. We therefore asked the opinion of a number of girls whose ways of living seemed typical of the group. Item by item the investigator talked over the year's budget, and the girl's own privations were clearly demonstrated when she explained that she could not afford to have any one do her washing for her but that it was very hard to have to do it herself after a long day's work, and that the wages ought to be big enough to cover it; or that she had never been able to buy a hot-water bag, but that every girl ought to have one; or that she walked to work and saved carfare, but that many girls lived too far away from their shop for that; or that she never had had enough money to go away for a vacation, but that a working girl needs the rest to keep her well. The composite picture of their estimates for the admitted necessities of a bare living for a week may be sketched by averaging their statements, as follows:

Expenses per week:

Board and lodging	$5.79
Clothes	2.00
Carfare	.60
Laundry	.50
Doctor, medicine, and dentist	.25
Total	$9.14

Note that the estimate makes no provision for recreation, stamps and stationery, newspapers, vacations, church contributions, dues to club or union, insurance, or savings, yet it amounts to

A Crowded Workroom on Broadway

Busy Season in a Third Avenue Shop

about $475 for the year, or a steady income of a little over $9.00 a week for a girl living alone. The actual cost of room and board was reported by 24 of the 40 women who were boarding. Ten, the largest group, paid between $5.00 and $6.00 a week, two between $6.00 and $7.00, and one $8.00, while five paid between $4.00 and $5.00, four between $3.00 and $3.50, and two between $2.00 and $3.00. Twenty-two boarded with private families, many of them with friends or relatives; eleven lived in working girls' boarding homes, more or less philanthropic in management, and seven lived in furnished rooms. The majority of the girls, 212, lived at home. Of these, only three were heads of households, six lived with their husbands, 138 belonged to families in which the father was living, 50 to homes of which the mother was the head, and 15 lived with brothers, sisters, or other relatives. These 15 were not boarding, but sharing expenses. Only six of the 136 reporting as to expenditures said that they contributed nothing to the home, while 26 gave part and 104 all their earnings.

In co-operative living in families the per capita cost may be less than if one boards, but it seems fair to say that this lower cost would be offset by the fact that in the majority of households the support of dependents must be shared by the wage-earners. Frequently the inadequacy of individual earnings is obscured by the pooling of the family wages. Of course, it is inevitable that the deficiency should be supplied by the other wage-earners or that the family standards be lowered. One milliner explained how she met the emergency of slack season. "We are a big family and I give all my money in. Then when it's slack, I don't. So it is different with me from what it is with a girl who is boarding." An Austrian, who earned a weekly rate of $11 with an annual income of $368, was boarding with a cousin to whom she paid $4.00 a week. "If you're living with strangers, it's hard when slack season comes," she said. Her ambition was to save enough to go home to Austria, but she said that all that she could do was to hope. Her margin for the year for all expenses except board had been $160. Yet she was earning almost exactly the amount ($365) which we have found to be the actual median annual income of milliners.

A trimmer and copyist in a wholesale shop had attained a wage of $10, but in slack season she took a position for $6.00, because, as she explained, she was helpless and needed the work and employers took advantage of her. She was living with an aunt who charged her $4.00 for board, but when her pay was reduced she charged her nothing. The girl was twenty-two years old and had had seven years' experience and ought to have been able to earn her living. She said that her aunt would not be able to support her partially very much longer.

A girl earning $9.00, which is commonly considered a living wage in New York, was nominally employed in the shop throughout the year, losing thirteen whole weeks, however, and a few days at other times. Her earnings for the year amounted to $336, with an average of $8.60 for the 39 weeks on the payroll. She was boarding in New York, but in slack season she visited her mother in the country. She said that she could not get along at all without this help from her mother.

A Russian of twenty-four lived with her aunt, to whom she paid $3.50 for room and meals. She can earn $12 a week, but the slack season in her "place of business," as she expressed it, had been unusually long and she had earned $304 in the year. At the time of the interview, the last day of July, she had been at work three weeks, and she was trying to pay back the accumulated debts of the slack season. For instance, she was giving her aunt $8.00 a week. "When I've paid what I owe for board, it will be slack season again," she said.

The ways of living in order to make the wages go as far as possible are not always comfortable. Three dollars a week for sleeping on a couch in the dining room of the family with whom she boarded, with the privilege of keeping her clothes in a closet in another room, was all that one girl could spare, even though she earned $12 a week. She had lost seven weeks because of slack season, and twenty-three through illness, and her income had been $185 in the year. She was in debt for part of her board.

Another boarded with a friend, paying $5.00 a week, which she said would be an unfair estimate of what others must pay, since her friend charged her less than if she had been a stranger. In return for the low rate charged she helped with the housework. As a further means of economy she made her own clothes.

Two sisters, both of them milliners, lived in one furnished room at $10 a month. They took care of it themselves and had milk and rolls for breakfast. They bought lunches near the shop and dinners for 30 cents in the neighborhood where they lived. It cost them $5.00 a week apiece for food and rent of room. One of them had been on the payroll fifty-two weeks, earning $503, and the other, fifty-one weeks, receiving $357. They were not able to save, as they were sending money home to their mother in Russia.

Several girls spoke of the influence of the trade on their ideas of the way they would like to live. Seeing all the new styles develops a wish for better clothes and some of them declared that this ambition, with the wages too low to satisfy it, was responsible for some immoral conditions. Sometimes the position itself requires a somewhat expensive style of dress, especially for designers or forewomen who frequently meet customers.

Not the least significant feature of the millinery trade is the great difference in family status and standards among the girls in the industry. An illustration of these differences is the contrast between the girls who have been described and a milliner whose family always spent the summer in the country and who prolonged her vacation into the autumn from choice and not from the necessities of the season. She had earned a weekly wage of $12, and the fact that her yearly income amounted to only $248 was no hardship to her. Whether the presence of these girls in the shops affects the wage scale is an open question. They are comparatively few in number and, as one of them declared, "I don't have to work, but I want just as high wages as the other girls. That's human nature." Probably their significance is not so much in the possibility of their underbidding those who are harder pressed by economic needs as in the fact that their working at all is an indication of the much larger potential labor supply for this industry. Were it more difficult to secure workers, the necessity for lengthening the seasons would be more apparent to employers. In this way, especially, a large supply of workers, probably larger than necessary, affects earnings.

The supply in relation to the demand varies, of course, with the seasons. In a retail shop we were told in a certain week in March that milliners were scarce, but that in the following week the wholesale season would be over and then there would be too many. At about the same date another employer said: "If I had advertised to-day, I could have a dozen girls to-morrow." On Division Street we were told by an employer that it was hard to find workers in the busy season, but that in dull season the girls would work for anything he wished to pay them. At a Fifth Avenue establishment, whose reputation attracts many experienced workers, we were told that apprentices are in most demand, since girls of sixteen, the minimum age in this shop, do not wish to work for $2.00 a week. One of the wholesalers, who helps his out-of-town customers find trimmers, said that although he sometimes had 25 calls a day for girls to go out of the city, he rarely had any trouble in finding satisfactory ones. In the last few seasons, especially, the supply had been greater than the demand. Trimmers who had earned $35 and $40 were glad then to take $25. Trimming hats free at the ribbon counter in department stores is hurting the trimmer's chance in the shop.

A woman who runs a successful retail shop gave similar testimony, that in the last three or four years many expert milliners had found it difficult to find positions. She attributed this condition to a change of style to simpler and smaller hats which require less work to construct, so that a designer can make them with very little assistance. She thought the change in style was due to the automobile.

On the whole, the workers agreed with the employers' statements on this point. "They can get all the good milliners they need," said one woman of long experience. "I don't know what we will do," said another, who had been a member of the milliners' union and much interested in trade conditions. "We will have to learn to be carpenters or plumbers. There is no money in millinery and no work anyway."

On the other hand, some employers complained of a great lack of efficient workers. "Out of a hundred girls here in my shop," said a member of one of the larger wholesale firms, "not 10 could make a hat if you gave them the material and told them to do it, without fussing and wasting their time and ours. They would not know how to go ahead unless somebody showed them. Everything has to be cut out for them. If a yard and a half goes in the rosette on one side and a yard and a quarter on the other, the milliner gets it cut just right for her." Another in a large shop declared that "workers are plentiful but efficiency is rare." On Division Street an employer told us that to avoid the scarcity of experienced workers, and especially to avoid paying high wages, he engages girls two weeks before the season begins. "If I wait till the season is on," he said, "the girls can make their own price."

HIRING WORKERS AND DETERMINING WAGES

Perhaps because of diversity of conditions in different shops and because of the unstable character of the occupation, no organization exists to voice the common interests of any large group of the workers. A very small band of foreign-born girls in wholesale shops have called themselves a union for several years, but so far they cannot be said to have made any impression upon the industry. The history of the union is interesting. It seems to have been the outgrowth of the social philosophy of a group of Russian Jewish girls who happened to be milliners, rather than a concerted movement developing naturally in the trade.

It was about 1905 that two of these girls brought together 60 others and formed the Milliners' Union. Later it was affiliated with the Industrial Workers of the World. The members tried hard to gain new recruits. They talked to the girls in the shops and made speeches on street corners, for which they were arrested at least once, if not oftener, for lack of a proper permit. They published leaflets for distribution and held mass meetings. In the hope of appealing to their more frivolous fellow workers they planned dances and gave entertainments. One of these, attended by the investigators, had a most delightful program of recitations and very beautiful music rendered by some of the artistic foreigners of the East Side. At one time the union grew to include more than 200 members, but later it dwindled away, because the chief leader had tuberculosis and went to Colorado. About 10 or 12 enthusiastic followers remained to hold their weekly meetings for reports on shop conditions and plans for organization, but they encountered overwhelming discouragement. Their one hope seemed to be that "some day conditions in the trade will get so bad that the girls will come to realize the necessity of a union."

The winter of 1916–17 witnessed an attempt to realize this hope. It was reported to the American Federation of Labor at its convention in Baltimore in November, 1916, that the cloth hat and cap makers had met with success in organizing the straw hat makers. These girls were workers in the manufacture of hats at wholesale as distinct from trimming in retail or wholesale establishments. In January, 1917, the locals responsible for the organization of the straw hat makers called a mass meeting for the purpose of organizing the milliners into an effective working body, but whether this renewed effort will meet with success is a problem of the future.

It is exceedingly difficult to organize a trade in which the majority of the workers are together but half the year, especially when even that half is divided into two quarters and between these periods the milliners are no longer milliners, but salesgirls, artificial flowers makers, operators on clothing or, indeed, workers in whatever other occupations they can find.*

* Only one benefit association was found, and that had been organized by the firm in an establishment in which millinery is but one of many departments and was not for milliners only. The employes pay dues of 10 cents a week if they are senior members, and five if they are juniors; and the benefits in case of sickness are $6.00 a week for seniors and $3.00 for juniors. A death benefit of $50 for seniors and $25 for juniors is also paid by the organization. In other establishments the employers, questioned about benefit associations, replied almost uniformly that with so long a slack season, during which the workers are scattered and dues could not be collected, it would be impossible to manage any such organization. This is a significant comment on the disorganized state of the industry.

Since the workers have no organization through which to bargain with their employers, the question of how wages are determined resolves itself into a discussion of the terms on which each milliner, acting for herself alone, secures and keeps a position, and how her employer decides what her wages shall be. Signs at street entrances of the shops and advertisements in newspapers are the two chief means of making known vacancies in the workroom. Former employes are notified by post card or sometimes by telephone when the season begins and they are needed. Through them, also, new workers are often secured. Some firms, whose reputations are famous in the trade, never advertise nor hang up signs, but depend entirely upon the personal application of milliners who come to them in search of positions because of the great asset which employment in one of these high grade establishments is supposed to be in their careers.

In some shops the hiring is done by the forewoman, and in others by a member of the firm. The usual practice in the wage bargain is to try a girl for two or three days or longer "to find out what she is worth." The method described in one shop is typical of several. A girl is engaged at the wage she specifies, and then, after a few days' trial, if she has not impressed the forewoman as being worth what she asks, she is offered a lower wage. If she refuses it she loses her position, but she is paid for the work she has done at the rate she has named. "They usually stay for what they are offered," said one employer.

That the labor contract is often merely a chance to work for an uncertain wage during an uncertain period is illustrated by the receipt which one firm has its employes sign on pay day each week. "Received from Blank and Company full settlement for salary and all claims to date. We also understand that no agreement or contract exists between Blank and Company and ourselves other than we are engaged by the week, but if we leave or are discharged, we are to be paid only for the actual time we have worked."

After the initial bargain is made, advancement depends quite as much upon chance as in the beginning. "If a girl asks for a raise, we give it to her if we have to," said one milliner in a prosperous establishment. It is the practice to keep track at each table of the time taken to make a hat as well as the cost of materials, but this is not a record of individual efficiency. That the experience of the employer in such matters, or the casual observation of a girl's work by the forewoman, is a sufficiently accurate method of determining wage rates seems to be the common belief in the trade. It is, however, but the rule-of-thumb method which the efficiency engineers are trying to persuade manufacturers in other industries to abandon in favor of the more scientific plan of keeping individual records. Of course, for piece workers, earnings are determined by the number of hats they trim, but the same hit-or-miss method described in estimating wages applies here in the fixing of rates per piece. In fact, our questions about methods of determining rates of pay and plans for promotion usually puzzled the employers. Their most frequent reply was that it was impossible to standardize wages in millinery. It is probable that this was really a confession of failure to grapple with the problem.

As might be expected from this chaotic method of bargaining, the wage scales vary greatly from firm to firm even in the same branch of the trade. Table 48, on page 228, showing the median wage for each firm, reveals the fact that the median is $6.25 in one wholesale shop and $12.50 in another; $5.00 in one retail establishment and $13.58 in another. Still more striking was the difference between five retail shops which have been discussed before because of the contrasts in the regularity of work which they offer, while their clientèle and their product are much alike. (Table 17, p. 102.) Table 22 shows the differences in average weekly earnings during the year in these shops.

In these five shops, all located in the fashionable millinery center, the median of average earnings actually varied from $6.60 to $13.58. This difference between firms is one of the most important facts brought out in this, as in other wage investigations. Certainly it indicates that competition does not necessarily result in uniformity in work conditions. It shows also that low wages are not essential to success. The fact that some successful firms are able to maintain conditions which are favorable for the workers demonstrates the possibility for them all.

TABLE 22.—AVERAGE WEEKLY EARNINGS IN SINGLE ESTABLISHMENTS DURING THE CALENDAR YEAR 1913, FOR WOMEN EMPLOYED IN FIVE LEADING MILLINERY ESTABLISHMENTS IN NEW YORK CITY

Average weekly earnings	Women employed in establishment					All women
	A	B	C	D	E	
Less than $6	34	36	32	18	17	137
$6 and less than $8	11	14	9	6	4	44
$8 and less than $10	17	12	8	6	15	58
$10 and less than $15	72	15	46	21	24	178
$15 or more	23	5	18	32	12	90
Total	157	82	113	83	72	507
Median average earnings[a]	$11.24	$6.60	$11.08	$13.58	$10.00	$10.37

[a] See footnote b, p. 83, for formula. In computing the medians for weekly wage rates and earnings in this and in succeeding tables, the calculation has been based on more minute groupings than are presented in the report, in order to secure greater accuracy in the result.

HOURS AND OTHER CONDITIONS OF WORK

It is important, of course, in relation to wages to know the hours of labor. Table 23 gives this information.

Of the 57 firms* investigated in the payroll

* Of the 149 establishments included in the entire investigation, 92 which were covered in the first section of this study were investigated before the New York fifty-four-hour law went into effect, and hence are not included in the tabulation of hours of work.

study, only six, employing 209 workers in their millinery workrooms in busy season, had a working week of less than fifty hours. The largest group, 22 firms, employing 906 millinery workers, had a schedule of fifty-one or fifty-one and a fraction, but less than fifty-two hours. The group working normally up to the exact limit the law allows, that is, fifty-four hours a week, numbered 16 firms with a force of 810 milliners.

TABLE 23.—WEEKLY HOURS OF WORK IN MILLINERY ESTABLISHMENTS INVESTIGATED IN PAYROLL STUDY AND MAXIMUM NUMBER OF WOMEN EMPLOYED. 1913

Weekly hours of work	Establishments	Maximum number of women employed	
		Number	Per cent
Less than 48 hours	2	93	3.7
48 hours and less than 49	2	31	1.2
49 hours and less than 50	2	85	3.3
50 hours and less than 51	2	135	5.3
51 hours and less than 52	22	906	35.5
52 hours and less than 53	3	57	2.2
53 hours and less than 54	8	433	17.0
54 hours	16	810	31.8
Total	57	2,550	100.0

The firms working less than fifty-four hours may legally increase the hours of employment in busy season, but for those whose normal schedule is up to the legal limit, any overtime constitutes a violation of the law. As to the extent of such violations of law in the millinery trade it is difficult for anyone to speak with authority. Evidence is not easy to secure. Even the payroll does not give conclusive facts, since it does not show the hours of work of piece workers. Nevertheless, some instances of overtime appeared in the records of week workers' earnings. In one large retail shop the payroll showed overtime in four successive weeks in the spring, varying from one to three nights a week for different workers. The compensation for one night's work, usually until 9 p. m., was half a day's pay. As the normal working week in this shop was fifty-one hours, three nights of overtime of three hours each night for a worker brought her week up to sixty hours, or six hours more than the law allows. Generally the retail shops insisted that they had very little overtime, perhaps a half hour or so occasionally to finish one hat, and that even in such cases only one or two girls would stay to do the work.

Perhaps the worst offenders in the matter of hours are the small retail shops with a neighborhood trade which reaches its maximum in the evening, especially on Saturday night. Both saleswomen and milliners must stay late to catch every possible bit of custom. It is a common practice to keep the store open until ten o'clock or later on Saturday night, and in the busy season it is usually open until nine the other five nights. We found that these were considered the usual hours in such small shops, and no one thought of paying extra for evening work. Usually latitude was allowed in coming later in the morning. One employer in a neighborhood store said that on five days in the week his shop was generally run at a loss, and that he counted on the Saturday rush to make good this loss and to yield a profit. He deplores the increasing stringency of laws regulating hours of work, and contends that it interferes seriously with the convenience of working-class shoppers.

Overtime is probably very frequent and often excessive among piece workers in wholesale shops, but as we have already explained, for piece workers it does not appear as a separate item on the payrolls. In some instances we were told by employers that it was the regular practice to work overtime on busy days until half-past eight at night, with a half hour for supper, or if the girls prefer to omit the time for supper, they could stop work at eight, making a ten and a half hour day. In other cases they worked until nine o'clock. In some wholesale shops home work is a substitute for overtime, the girls taking home a bundle of work and returning it to the shop in the morning. The work may be the making of hats or of such trimmings as rosettes and bows. Other employers, however, whose products are of high grade, say that the danger of losing materials and of having the work badly done while unsupervised is so great as to make it impracticable to give out work in this way. Occasional instances of it, never-

Practicing for Home Work for a Wholesale Shop

Open Evenings

theless, were discovered even in the most expensive shops.

Of workroom conditions no general statement can be made, since conditions differ so greatly in different establishments. Perhaps the most serious conditions are found in the small stores on the street level with workrooms in the rear. Ventilation and light are both seriously inadequate. In one of these, for instance, the workroom windows looked out on a very narrow back yard flanked by a fifteen-story building. The milliners worked all day by electric light. Some of the large Broadway lofts are equally lacking in provisions for light and air, or for comfort. In one no lockers were provided and the hats and coats hung on the walls of the workroom. In contrast, another firm had arranged an attractive dressing room, with neat, white woodwork, and with all the other workroom conditions, toilet arrangements, lighting, ventilation, and space, most carefully planned.

The state has already established minimum conditions of sanitation and hygiene in shops and factories, and it has also limited the hours of women's work, all of these laws applying to millinery establishments. It may be that the next step will be the establishment of wage standards.

CHAPTER VI

LEARNING THE TRADE

LEARNING the trade may seem to be a subject which belongs at the beginning rather than near the end of the description of an industry. In reality, learning means more than the first steps at entrance into an occupation. It means adjustment to all the complex conditions which affect both learners and experienced workers. Fruitful discussion of the period of apprenticeship and the methods of developing a new recruit into an expert demands full knowledge of the trade itself, what it requires of its workers and what it offers in return. That millinery is a skilled industry, that it is not concentrated in one locality, but is a resource for women in many communities, that its demands vary greatly in different branches of the trade, with speed as an essential in some of the wholesale shops and accuracy, delicacy, and taste the desiderata in the finer tasks of retail work, and most important of all, that the range of wages is wide and rates comparatively high, but that the long, slack seasons reduce the income for many workers below the amount which seems necessary for wholesome living,—these are all facts not only important for the child who is choosing a trade, but pertinent for the educator who is considering plans for industrial education.

Millinery is one of the trades in which the term apprentice is still used. Apprenticeship, however, is not a formal matter. No contract is made between the child or its parents and the employer. A learner is engaged, but no period of training is agreed upon in advance.

Not all firms are willing to employ untrained workers. Of 148 reporting on this point, 42 refuse to employ them, 11 employ them occasionally, and 95 employ them regularly. Among these 95 were 76 retail shops. It is in retail that the learner most often finds her opportunity. Of the 47 wholesale firms reporting on this subject, 23 engaged no apprentices, 19 employed them regularly, and 5 occasionally, while of the 101 retail shops, only 19 give no opportunity at any time to learners. The absence of learners in many wholesale shops is doubtless due in part to the fact that modern factory methods of machine processes and subdivision of work are characteristic of wholesale, whereas hand work and the older methods of organization still obtain in retail.

Methods of training differ in different shops. Sometimes the young workers are merely errand girls. "It's all outside work, learning is," said one of them. "You run errands for eight months." In the larger shops the plan of organization of the force in groups with a trimmer at the head of each table and six or seven makers and improvers and generally one apprentice working under her direction, results often in excellent training. The learner has the advantage of working under constant supervision, while at the same time she sees the entire process from the making of the bandeau and the preparation of the lining, which are usually her duties, to the final trimming. One girl described the course of learning by saying that "the trimmer shows the maker, the maker shows the improver, and the improver shows the apprentice." Under such a system the efficiency of the training depends upon the teaching ability of the trimmer at the head of the table, and therefore the opportunity for an apprentice varies from table to table, even in the same establishment. The line of demarcation between learner and improver, and improver and maker, is not very distinct. Gradually the apprentice learns to do more and more of the work of preparing the hat for the trimmer, and she becomes an improver, and then a preparer, and then a maker. Although the length of the apprenticeship period is not clearly defined, it is generally agreed in the higher grade establishments that it takes about three or four seasons, that is, two years, to train a maker. In one of the best shops we were told that it takes at least two seasons to become an improver, and four or five years to be a competent maker.

In the high grade wholesale establishments the process of training is very like that in retail. In others, the difference in the type of product results

Forewoman Criticizing Work

in different requirements which affect the learner's opportunity. If the chief task of trimming be the putting in of a lining and the sewing on of a bow or a quill in a ready-to-wear hat, the demand is for speed, and inexperienced girls may repeat essentially the same process until they become proficient. Obviously this is not comparable with the training given in a retail shop. One employer explained that the only way he could make the practice of taking learners at $4.00 or $5.00 a week really pay, would be to let the learner make one kind of crown or one kind of frame the entire season. We were told in another shop that some of the girls bring younger sisters and divide their piecework earnings with them so that the firm is not obliged to take time "to bother with learners." One girl with whom we talked had worked with her sister in this way for a year, her sister receiving their combined earnings from the firm. In another wholesale establishment the employer said that young girls were employed for finishing and lining hats but that she did not consider that these were learners. They are expected to continue at this process indefinitely.

The complaint was made frequently concerning both wholesale and retail shops that it was hard for a learner to advance, that she was not given an opportunity to learn all the processes, and that an employer would lay off apprentices after one season and take on others so as to keep the payroll smaller. "They would not advance me," said one girl, who after five years in the millinery workroom of a department store was getting only $5.00, but who was paid $10 at once in her next position in a Fifth Avenue retail shop. "For two years they kept me on errands and halos" (a species of bandeau).

"There's an awful lot of apprentices in our shop," said one girl. "They work six months for 50 cents a week. We makers teach them. It is not good for us. They are supposed to learn everything in six months, and then they are doing the same work we do at less wages and when the dull season comes they keep them and lay us off. Some of them are pretty well off too. They get an allowance from home." This shop was the subject of much criticism among both employers and workers, and in our study later of the payroll we found evidence of the fifty-cent wage, but by that time the force had become much smaller, and the business was not prospering. As an illustration of the possible abuse of the apprentice idea, however, its history had significance.

Apprenticeship systems in millinery in at least seven foreign countries were represented among the girls whom we interviewed—Russia, France, Ireland, Roumania, Austria, Canada, and England. One of the Russians had learned the trade there because she was planning to come to the United States, and her father who had come before her had written that it was a good trade in New York. She paid for her apprenticeship and worked a year and a half without wages, but to her bitter disappointment she found the methods so different in the cheap retail shop on Orchard Street and later in wholesale establishments, that it was like learning all over again. In Russia, she said, a good milliner may spend a whole day making a hat, but here everything must be done in a hurry.

One of the girls trained in Ireland was more fortunate, as she became a copyist at $11 a week in a high grade retail shop as soon as she arrived. Doubtless her greater success as compared with the Russian was due in part to the fact that she was not obliged to learn a new language. A foreign-born girl who speaks no English could not find work in the better grade retail shops. Her only opportunities would be in the wholesale trade or in the small neighborhood shops, and if her training had been in high grade establishments abroad, the work here would seem like a new trade to her. In addition, however, this Irish girl's success seems to have been due to very careful training. She had worked without wages for two years in Belfast, then for three years she was employed in another shop there, attaining a wage of 11 shillings and finally she developed her own trade at home. Another girl had had a long and thorough apprenticeship in Ireland, learning to do all kinds of work, even blocking hats, which would be considered a separate trade here. It was perhaps the Parisian girls who described the most careful plans for apprenticeship, with thorough and exacting practice in all the processes of millinery, with the great advantage, besides, of acquiring a sense of the famous French taste in matters of dress. It is by no means uncommon there for the girl's family to pay for her apprenticeship.

Low wages for learners in New York were defended by employers on the ground that the experienced workers must take their valuable time to teach, and that the learner's work is not worth much to the firm. That the general level of learners' wages was not high is indicated in Table 24.

TABLE 24.—FIRST WEEKLY WAGES RECEIVED IN RETAIL OR WHOLESALE MILLINERY ESTABLISHMENTS BY WORKERS INTERVIEWED AT HOME

First weekly wages	Women who began millinery work in		All women
	Retail	Wholesale	
No wages	52	16	68
Wages of			
Less than $2.00	38	9	47
$2.00 and less than $2.50	19	11	30
$2.50 and less than $3.00	9	3	12
$3.00 and less than $3.50	14	13	27
$3.50 and less than $4.00	3	2	5
$4.00 and less than $5.00	2	6	8
$5.00 and less than $6.00	3	5	8
$6.00 and less than $7.00	3	5	8
$7.00 or more	1	1	2
Total	144	71	215[a]

[a] Of the 252 women interviewed at home, 12 who began work in the retail branch of the trade and 19 who began in wholesale did not state initial wages, 4 did not give information as to the branch of the trade in which they began work, and 2 failed to state either fact.

The table shows the beginning wage of 215 of the 252 girls with whom we talked. Because of the differences in the length of their experience it relates to varying periods of time, and only a few were learners at the time of the interview. Of the 215 reporting on this point, as many as 68 had received no pay when they first began, and of these, 52 worked in retail. The median for the whole number, including those without pay, was $1.68. The median for those receiving wages was $2.44. Our payroll study showed that the median actual earnings for apprentices was $3.39.* This probably corroborates the opinion quite frequently expressed that the wages of apprentices are higher than they used to be, as the group interviewed at home includes a number who were learners several years ago. The fact that in our payroll study we investigated chiefly the larger establishments, whereas the girls whom we interviewed had learned in many different types of shops, may also be a factor in the difference. In our entire inquiry, however, we discovered very few shops in which apprentices are at present employed without pay. We found one instance where an employer was paid to teach an apprentice. This was in a retail shop on Second Avenue. The girl's family paid $10 for a year's apprenticeship, but the employer broke his word and discharged her after nine months.

The girls who reported higher wages than the average as learners had had previous training in

* Table 40, p. 260.

needlework or had had an opportunity to know something about millinery before beginning to work in a shop. For instance, a Russian girl had been a saleswoman in her sister's millinery shop on the lower East Side, and this gave her a chance to learn about the trade, so that she went to work not as a learner but as a preparer in a Division Street shop at $5.00 a week. After two months she found work in a Broadway wholesale establishment at $10 a week. Hers was an unusual experience. In another instance the girl's mother had had a millinery business and she began as an improver at a wage of $5.00. Another said that she did not begin as a learner because she had always been interested in millinery and had "made hats for fun" so often that she, too, was ready for a five-dollar wage. Another girl learned cheap wholesale processes by helping her sister make hats at home for a contractor. Of the 242 girls who gave information about the kind of work done in their first positions in millinery, 189 had been learners and 18 had been errand girls, with no sharp line of demarcation between these two groups. Of the others, 11 had been preparers, 10 improvers, 5 copyists, 1 maker, 3 stock girls, 2 saleswomen, 1 shopper, 1 operator, and 1 frame maker. The majority of the 252 girls, 144, began work in retail shops, 12 in department stores where the work was also for the retail trade, and 90 in wholesale (six not reporting).

It is noteworthy that a large group, 203, began

Training an Apprentice

work in millinery as soon as they left school, while 24 others were in some other division of the sewing trades.* The majority, 163, were not yet sixteen years old when they began to work for wages.

Of the 196 who told us how they found their first positions in millinery, 70 had been placed by friends, 35 by relatives, 60 had answered advertisements, 24 had applied directly to an employer, in some instances after seeing a sign at the door announcing that workers were needed, 6 had found work through the recommendation of a trade school which they had attended, and 1 through an employment bureau.

Tables 25, 26, and 27 show in order the age when these girls left school, the last schools attended, and for those who had been pupils in New York City public schools, the grade reached.

TABLE 25.—AGE AT LEAVING SCHOOL OF MILLINERY WORKERS INTERVIEWED AT HOME

Age at leaving school	Women
Under 14 years	48
14 years	95
15 years	53
16 years	24
17 years	6
18 years or more	2
Total	228[a]

[a] Of the 252 women interviewed at home, 6 had never attended school and 18 did not state age at leaving school.

* Four did not report on this point, and 21 had been in other occupations.

TABLE 26.—LAST DAY SCHOOL ATTENDED BY MILLINERY WORKERS INTERVIEWED AT HOME

Last day school attended	Women
New York City school	
Public	141
Parochial	15
All other	1
Total	157
Schools in United States outside New York City	11
Foreign school	75
None	6
Grand total	249[a]

[a] Of the 252 women interviewed at home, three did not give information as to the last day school attended.

TABLE 27.—GRADE AT LEAVING SCHOOL FOR MILLINERY WORKERS WHO LAST ATTENDED DAY SCHOOL IN A NEW YORK CITY PUBLIC SCHOOL

Grade at leaving school	Women
4th grade or lower	1
5th grade	5
6th grade	22
7th grade	30
8th grade	18
Elementary school graduate	40
High school	
Non-graduate	13
Graduate	1
Total	130[a]

[a] Of the 141 women who last attended day school in a New York City public school, 11 did not state their grade at leaving school.

Of the 234 reporting, six had never attended school and 48 had left even before they were fourteen years old. As many as 148 left at the age of fourteen or fifteen and only 32 stayed until they were sixteen or older. Seventy-five had attended foreign schools and 157 had last attended school in New York City, 141 of these having been public school pupils. Of these 141, the number who reported the grade reached was 130, of whom 54 had graduated from elementary school, 14 of these going to high school, but only one graduating. Twenty-eight left before reaching the seventh grade.

A surprisingly large group, however, had not been content with this schooling, 151 reporting attendance at schools or classes after going to work, and 21 of these taking more than one supplementary course of this kind. Thus 100 reported attendance at public evening elementary schools, 25 at evening high schools, 24 at trade schools, 7 at business schools, and 16 at other schools or classes.

Two facts stand out as perhaps the most significant in all these figures. The time for schooling is brief for milliners as it is for the great majority of girls working in trades, but they welcome opportunities for additional training during the wage-earning period.

TRAINING CLASSES FOR MILLINERS

The millinery trade affords an excellent example of the problem of industrial education for girls. With dressmaking it is usually the first choice among trades to be included in the curriculum of a trade school. The Manhattan Trade School for Girls made it one of its four departments when the school was started in 1902. The Boston Trade School has had a millinery department from the beginning. Following the educational survey of Cleveland in 1916, the organization of a trade school to teach millinery, dressmaking, and machine operating was advocated.* As a result of the Minneapolis Survey a two years' course of training, with three months' probationary period at the beginning, was planned in conference with employers of milliners, dressmakers, machine operators, saleswomen, and nurses.†

In 1908–09, in the beginning of our investigation, we visited no less than 62 classes in millinery in New York City, and it is probable that we did not exhaust the list. The majority of these classes aimed merely to teach girls to make their own hats, but some of the best organized, such as the courses in Pratt Institute, the Clara de Hirsch Home or the Manhattan Trade School, were definitely seeking to train workers for the trade, and it was trade training and not merely training for home use which was recommended in the Cleveland Survey and the Minneapolis Survey.

* Bryner, Edna: Dressmaking and Millinery, p. 127. Cleveland Education Survey Report. Cleveland, 1916.

† Report of the Minneapolis Survey for Vocational Education, pp. 432–435. National Society for the Promotion of Industrial Education, Bulletin 21. January 1, 1916.

It was made a part of an agreement proposed between schools and employers that at the end of this course a wage of no less than $8.00 should be paid those who had had this training.

The arguments in favor of including millinery in a scheme of industrial courses for women are clearly set forth in the Cleveland Survey. A large proportion of wage-earning girls find their opportunities for employment in the sewing trades of which millinery is a part. Millinery is an occupation in which training is possible and desirable. It demands practice in the use of the needle, knowledge of line and color, and skill in adapting materials to their uses. It offers opportunities ahead for increasing skill and developing aptitude. A preliminary ground work of training makes possible the development of greater skill under shop conditions.

Nevertheless, although these underlying facts are as true in New York as in Cleveland or Minneapolis or Boston or many other cities, our interviews with employers and with workers in New York, supplemented by visits to 62 millinery classes,* raised some interesting questions as to the desirability of organizing classes to give preliminary training to future milliners.

It was clear in the first place that millinery classes were not popular either among employers or workers.† "In the schools they miss the point of it somehow," said a successful owner of a retail shop. "There are a thousand little things the girls

* Barrows, Alice P., and Van Kleeck, Mary: How Girls Learn the Millinery Trade. *The Survey*, XXIV: 105–113 (April 16, 1910).

† Both employers and workers spoke very bitterly of the schools run for profit, some of which attract pupils by the promise of an equipment quite impossible to supply in a brief period.

get in a shop that they don't get anywhere else." "The mechanical part of millinery can be acquired through training, but trimming is more and more an art," said another employer in one of the best of the retail shops. "The schools teach girls to measure too exactly. They are never well trained for work in an establishment of this kind." "Trade schools are not successful because they do not deal directly with the business," said an employer in a wholesale shop. "The fundamental purpose of business is to make money. To make money you have to get out the goods. To get out the goods you have to give people what they want and to do that you have to deal directly with the customers." "Conditions change so that I would not myself know how to plan a course," said another, and the same idea was expressed by the woman who said that a course was not feasible because "millinery is different every year." "Trade schools teach you too much," said one of the workers; "for instance, just how much material you will need for each part and how to measure everything you need. But in a shop you never need to cut your own materials. It is always done for you." Another worker declared that "classes in the school are not so carefully supervised as the work in a shop. In the schools the classes are too large. In a shop each girl's work is watched and she is often obliged to do it over." Yet an apprentice in a shop who was also attending an evening class in millinery said that she was learning more in the school than in the shop, because "in the school they have more time to show you how to do the work."

Such criticisms, which were very frequent, relate more to the methods adopted in the schools than to the more fundamental question of whether it is desirable to give any preliminary trade training to future milliners. Several of the more thoughtful girls were quite emphatic in their disapproval of a too rapid increase in numbers in an already overcrowded trade. "There are too many milliners looking for work," said one girl of twelve years' experience. "If trade schools train too many, their training will not bring them higher wages because the increased numbers will keep the wages down." She added, however, that trades should be taught in the evening schools to enable girls already at work to learn the things which they are not taught in shops.

Her comments, like those of several others, clearly suggest the current idea that through offering equipment in a few trades only, a system of industrial education may complicate the problems of an industry. At present, one of the few checks against too excessive irregularity of employment in any trade is the difficulty of securing competent workers and the consequent necessity for retaining the force as long as possible. On the other hand, the presence of a large supply of labor enables employers to meet the problem of short and irregular seasons by offering employment for brief periods. As millinery is an attractive trade, interesting and socially desirable, as it is also one of the traditional pursuits of women and within the reach of the many who have had some practice at least in handling a needle, it has about it always a potential supply of labor in the groups of women and girls who may be persuaded by a very slight inducement to become wage-earners. Moreover, because of its attractions, the occupation appeals to a disproportionately large number of girls who know that they must earn their own living. A large number of classes offering training to equip women to find positions in millinery would, it is argued, aggravate unduly conditions tending already to increase the supply of workers in the trade, and to that extent to encourage employers to shorten the period of employment. Statistical evidence as to such a result is lacking, however.

Such an argument applies not to all forms of trade training, but merely to the so-called preliminary trade school which offers courses to equip workers for wage-earning positions. Unless such a scheme provides a place for practically all of the occupations of the community, it is open to the objection of encouraging an artificial selection of vocations on the part of its pupils. But the organization of schools or classes to give supplementary training to those who have already found their places in work is a suggestion which met with instant approval among some employers and workers. Evening classes, for instance, might train girls in a better understanding of color and

A Millinery Class in a Public Evening School
"You cannot do millinery at school desks"

Making Hats for the Wholesale Trade

line, supplementing the practice which they would be gaining at the same time in the workroom. "I don't think I have ever had a girl in my workroom who could see a line," said a retail milliner. "That is where we are weak in this country. We are not artists. You tell a girl a line is not right and she tells you the measurements are correct. A bow may have just the right measurement but because of a touch there will be a wrong curve."

Certainly it would seem to be true that if the movement for industrial education means anything, it means that the schools will some day offer to all the workers in the community the opportunity to learn whatever subject matter for teaching may be involved in their work. As one French girl expressed it, in defending the need for proper training for an occupation, "Pour vivre, il faut travailler; pour travailler, il faut savoir; pour savoir, il faut apprendre." The fact that there is a great deal to understand in millinery justifies its inclusion in a scheme of industrial training. What its place shall be in that scheme must be determined in the light of the effect of any given policy upon present trade standards and problems. These conditions must also determine the kind of advice to be given by teachers to those who aspire to be milliners. The policy of the Manhattan Trade School in describing fully the conditions of the trade, its short seasons and the low wages for beginners, to those who apply for enrollment in its millinery classes, and in transferring to other departments those who show no marked aptitude for millinery is an example of the way in which a public trade school may relate its practice to conditions in the trade in its own community.

It is not through trade classes only, however, that the schools may have an influence on the careers of milliners. To retain their pupils in school long enough to give opportunity for better development mentally and physically would in itself be a contribution to industrial efficiency. Statistical proof of the advantage of staying in school longer than the law requires is not easy to secure because the factors affecting wages are so complicated. But at least it is interesting to note the wage rates attained by those who began wage-earning before they were sixteen as compared with those who began at the age of sixteen or later. Table 28 shows these facts.

The table shows the median wage rate for each group according to years of experience as wage-earners. For the group as a whole and for each period of experience except one,—those who have worked twenty years or longer,—the advantage is with those who began when they were older. The exceptional group numbers only 18 and may be too small to serve as a basis for conclusions. The persistence of the difference in all the other groups in favor of those who did not go into industry until after they were sixteen indicates that for some reason higher earnings are attained if the beginning of the wage-earning period is postponed.

If true in any large number of industries, this fact adds further evidence of the constructive value of increasingly stringent child labor legislation.

TABLE 28.—MEDIAN WEEKLY WAGE RATES, BY AGE AT BEGINNING WORK AND YEARS SINCE BEGINNING WORK, FOR MILLINERY WEEK WORKERS ON CURRENT PAYROLL. 1914[a]

Years since beginning work	Median weekly wage rate of women who began work[b]	
	Under 16 years of age	At 16 years of age or more
Less than 1 year	$2.71	$3.33
1 year and less than 2	5.21	5.75
2 years and less than 3	6.62	6.94
3 years and less than 5	8.43	9.14
5 years and less than 10	12.22	13.14
10 years and less than 15	14.27	16.76
15 years and less than 20	17.50	21.50
20 years or more	20.00	15.00
Total	$10.75	$11.66

[a] For more detailed data, see Tables 50 A and 50 B, pp. 232–233.
[b] See footnote b, Table 10, p. 83.

SUMMARY

Millinery illustrates, then, some characteristic problems of industrial education. Its processes offer scope for taste and skill. As a craft with some elements of creative ability it affords a basis for a training course which would have a legitimate place in a school curriculum. From the practical point of view, success in preparing pupils to be good milliners depends upon the possibility either of reproducing trade conditions and trade requirements in a school or of forming such an alliance between school and shop as shall enable the school to supplement the practical experience of the shop with the additional training in line, color, and materials which the shop gives only indirectly. This additional training by the schools seems more necessary than the chance to practice the actual processes of hat trimming since millinery is still largely a hand industry and in the retail branches especially careful training is given in many establishments.

The outstanding problem in the trade which complicates the question of industrial training is the irregularity of employment, due chiefly to the short seasons, whereby wages are reduced to less than a living wage for a large majority of the workers. One element in this irregularity of employment is the apparently large supply of workers for which the millinery schools and classes are held partly responsible by both workers and employers in the trade. Another factor in irregularity is undoubtedly inefficiency. Employers make less effort to retain unsatisfactory workers. Those who lack skill or aptitude are likely to be drifters in the trade. A wise policy of industrial education could partly remedy this. No policy, however, would be wise which was not safeguarded carefully to prevent an unwise selection by girls with little aptitude for millinery, or by those who could not afford to work for low pay in so markedly seasonal an occupation. Moreover, any policy of industrial training in the public schools should be directly related to the efforts to control the standards in the trade through labor legislation, by preventing child labor, restricting the hours of work, regulating sanitary conditions, and possibly in time, providing machinery for collective bargaining to establish a higher standard of wages. Proposals regarding wage regulation will be discussed in the following chapter.

CHAPTER VII

PUBLIC CONTROL IN THE MILLINERY TRADE

PICTURESQUE, bizarre, or otherwise conspicuous though its products may be, the millinery trade has not yet captured the imagination of the public as an industry of any significance in the labor movement. It is chiefly in times of industrial conflict that now one trade and now another emerges from obscurity and challenges attention. Thus recently even the most indifferent citizen has learned many things about garment workers, about street-car conductors, and about brakemen on freight trains. Millinery, however, happens to be a trade which has never had a public hearing because widespread conflict is as yet unknown in it. For that very reason, indeed, employes in millinery shops need attention since they are part of the large group of workers in industry who have not yet learned to act together or even to express their needs in a common language. Their problems are often more urgent than are those in occupations in which common action by the workers has become habitual. In so far as control by the state may be exerted for the improvement of working conditions on a sound basis of public policy, action should be taken in time to avert unnecessary conflict and suffering. It was because some form of state control, at least in the matter of wages, might prove to be possible, that millinery was included among the occupations studied by the New York State Factory Investigating Commission in 1914.

After a remarkably thorough investigation of the wages of more than 100,000 men and women in four important industries besides millinery, and after careful inquiry into the cost of living, this official commission reported to the legislature which had created it that the lowest sum necessary for decent maintenance for a working woman in New York City is $9.00 a week, but that "one-half of all the wage-earners, including men and women, in the four principal industries investigated (confectionery, paper box, and shirt manufacturing and mercantile establishments) received less than $8.00 a week. Out of a total of 104,000 persons, one-eighth received less than $5.00, one-third less than $7.00, two-thirds less than $10 and only one-sixth are paid $15 or more."* In stores, no less than 54 per cent of the girls investigated received less than $7.50 a week, including commissions. In the shirt industry 54 per cent received less than $7.00 a week, while the records of box factories showed approximately

* New York State Factory Investigating Commission, Fourth Report, 1915. Vol. I, p. 34. For report on cost of living see Vol. IV, pp. 1461 ff.

the same proportion of underpaid workers. Less than $6.00 a week was the utmost that more than half the women and girls employed in making candy could earn.*

As a remedy the commission proposed a bill "to protect the health, morals and welfare of women and minors employed in industry by establishing a wage commission and providing for the determination of living wages for women and minors."†

The millinery workers with whom we discussed this proposal greeted it with enthusiasm and several of them justified their wish for improvement in the trade by writing out budgets showing how far their wages now fall short of a desirable standard. Bertha, for instance, was born in England of a Russian father and a French mother, and came to this country with her family, at the age of ten. Her father had become totally blind and her mother hoped to find better opportunities here to support the children. Bertha and her brother and sister went to school for five years until their mother died and their home was broken up. After a brief but good course in a millinery class maintained by a social organization, she began her career as a milliner in the wholesale trade. We interviewed her two years later, when she and her sister were boarding, sharing a small room with the daughter of the family with whom they lived. Bertha had never earned more than $7.00 a week in millinery. In the slack season which lasted at

* Ibid., pp. 35–36.

† Ibid., pp. 291 ff.

least three months, she had found employment as an operator in a handkerchief factory, where her maximum wages, by piece work, were $5.00 a week. Her total earnings in a year, allowing for irregular piece work in both trades and for loss of time between jobs, amounted approximately to $230. She had suffered from eye strain and had had no proper examination or care, and this made machine operating as well as millinery work especially difficult.

Her estimate of an adequate budget was $410 for the year, or approximately $8.00 a week, without any loss of time. To be sure, she included such luxuries as pictures of herself at $2.00, gifts to other people at $3.00, earrings, and six boxes of writing paper. She also included a weekly sum for laundry, which she must now do for herself after her day's work. In addition, experience had taught her that some money ought to be set aside for eyeglasses, which she needed and could not buy, for medicines, for dental care, and doctor's bills. In reality she received in a year $180 less than her estimate of her needs. Allowing $150 for the first big item of board and lodging, small as it was, because she lived with friends and had only a third of a room, she had but $80 left for all necessities in the year. Her sister and her friends were obliged to help her when work was slack. Yet in making out her budget she echoed the words of another milliner who sent us hers in writing with this statement: "I am just giving you an item of myself. Just what I think I need and nothing more." The girls themselves were as cautious in their statements as though they had been official investigators.

A thrifty German girl who had lost only a week and a half in the year, told us how she managed to live on $512 a year and save a little money. She paid $2.00 a week for a furnished room and by careful buying she managed to spend not more than $4.00 a week for her meals. She had been in this country only a year, and as she had brought with her a good supply of durable German clothing the necessary expenditures for that item were reduced. She makes all her own dresses and much of her underwear, buys remnants, some of them from factories where her friends work, and gets reductions in her own factory for millinery materials. She walks to work, does most of her own laundry, and cooks her own breakfast in her room. She estimated $425 as the necessary minimum. Her rate of pay is $12 a week, but when slack season comes, she is one of the few girls kept at work, although at a wage reduced to $8.00. The steadiness of her employment brings her annual income up to $512. The very thriftiness of her management makes her case the more convincing as showing that the estimate of $9.00 as the minimum living wage stands the test of experience. Moreover, this amount must be regularly received. Irregularity not only reduces income but makes management difficult, and gives a worker the feeling of dread and uncertainty which inevitably undermines health and efficiency.

Such is the evidence in story after story,—an inadequate wage and irregular employment keep the workers constantly near the margin where going into debt or obtaining assistance from others becomes necessary. After all, the cost of living is so much a matter of common knowledge, one of those subjects which makes the whole world kin, that extensive demonstration seems unnecessary. Perhaps it is sufficient to say that the fundamental needs of human beings are much alike whatever their trades may be, and that the cost of necessities does not vary downward to suit slender pocketbooks. Precarious incomes for workers whose wage at best is inadequate even when employment is steady, is, indeed, a grave social problem worthy of the consideration of state legislatures. The first step is to know the facts that we may thereby determine whether the community itself may exert any control over these conditions. It was the opinion of the Factory Investigating Commission of the first manufacturing state of this country that state control was possible and should be tried as a remedy for low wages.

A summary of the facts disclosed in our investigation of the millinery trade may serve to forecast the possible relation of such state control to the conditions discovered.

Uncle Sam, or Uncle Sam's wife, requires the services of 134,000 milliners. They are scattered throughout the country from Florida to Alaska, and from Maine to Texas, in order to be near their customers, but in no place are they so numerous as in New York City, which employs more than one in ten of their number. Moreover, no other place serves so many different communities. The products of New York millinery shops are shipped to every state in the Union. Its wholesale trade is much larger than its retail business. If the buyer be ultimately responsible for conditions of labor, as the Consumers' League has been telling us insistently for more than twenty-five years, then the responsibility for the conditions among New York milliners is as widespread as the country itself.

Shop conditions and even processes of work differ widely, not only between wholesale and retail work, but between different establishments in the same branch of the trade. Hat trimming is primarily a hand industry, and as such it lacks the standardizing influence of machinery. As a result it continues to be in part a home occupation, and a milliner working alone may compete more or less directly with a large establishment employing a hundred or more workers. To be sure, much of the work of our grandmothers' milliners, the sewing of straw and the making of velvet or silk or felt bonnets can now be done by machinery in factories, and certain tailored hats are almost entirely machine products, but trimming is still a hand process, and so long as women wear trimmed hats, milliners will continue to be subject to the conditions of hand workers. In the industry as a whole, these isolated workers in small shops or at home constitute a group whose conditions of employment cannot be controlled or standardized as could the work of a large shop. It is from the large shops, however, that the main currents of influence proceed. Moreover, the independent workers are all found in the retail branch of the trade. Wholesale work is entirely under shop control.

Two in five of the workers are under twenty-one, a proportion of young workers twice as large as in the allied trade of dressmaking. Three in five are native born, but the great majority are of foreign parentage. Many nationalities are represented. Russian Jews predominate, especially in the wholesale shops. Milliners as a whole come from homes varying greatly in standards of living, but in very rare cases are a girl's earnings unimportant in the maintenance of a home or in self-support away from home. Like the workers in other industries,* milliners are at work in order to earn a living, and to this end two conditions are essential,—a living wage, and steady work.

The great outstanding fact in the millinery

* In the summary of the federal report of 1907–08 on Woman and Child Wage-earners in the United States, it is stated that the industrial employment of girls sixteen years of age and over in families investigated was almost universal, and the report adds: "It seems certain that they are at work either because of economic necessity or because the standards of their class demand wage-earning from daughters as completely as from sons, or, which is probably the real situation, from both reasons combined."—U. S. Department of Labor, Bureau of Labor Statistics, Bulletin No. 175, p. 19.

trade is its appalling irregularity. Women wear two kinds of hats in a year, and this fact is reflected in two seasons, spring and fall,—a classification which still holds true for the sake of convenience, even though the present tendency seems to be to wear winter hats in August and summer hats in January. Moreover, the buying, and consequently the making, is thus concentrated in a period of approximately three months in spring and three months in the autumn. This means for milliners a search for work four times in every twelve months, twice in the busy seasons in millinery and twice in other occupations to fill in the dull time when for the majority of workers wage-earning in the millinery trade becomes impossible. In slightly less than half the year, twenty-five weeks, was the force in the shops investigated equal even to three-fourths or more of the maximum number employed in the busy season. Less than three in every hundred of the workers whose names were found on the payrolls received wages from one position for fifty-two weeks in the year. Forewomen had the longest periods of employment and apprentices the shortest, but no group from learners to designers escaped the constant shifting and the irregular work indicated in so reliable a document as the payroll.

These facts related to a single calendar year without regard to previous duration of employment in the same shop. Nevertheless, the questions answered by the workers themselves showed how frequent must be the shifts from shop to shop.

Only six in every hundred had had less than a year's experience in the trade, and yet as many as 31 in every hundred had been in the same shop less than a year. As many as 58 per cent could report that they had been milliners five years or longer, but only 22 per cent had been so long in one establishment.

Difficulty in finding positions in other shops in millinery or in other trades when millinery work is slack increases the amount of lost time and lost income. These are facts not shown on the payrolls. They are obtainable only from the workers themselves. Those whom we interviewed reported an average loss of nine weeks' income in the year, or 17 per cent of the normal working period. Some of this loss was due to illness, some to quitting work voluntarily and some to other causes of various kinds, but in the large majority of cases the biggest losses were due to slack season.

Rates of pay in millinery vary widely from 50 cents or nothing a week for learners to $150 for designers. The median rate for week workers as shown on the payrolls was $10.77, and the median actual earnings for both week workers and piece workers as revealed on the payroll of a single week was $9.69. Median rates varied from $4.14 for workers under sixteen to $20 for women of forty-five or older. But the higher wages are attained by only a very small proportion of the workers.

The wage rate is reduced by numerous small losses even while the worker's name continues to be carried on the payrolls. We were not content to know merely the rates or even the actual earnings for one week, and so we pursued the inquiry further, figuring for each worker on the payrolls at any time in the calendar year, the average weekly wage in her pay envelopes in any one shop. This showed that half the workers averaged less than $8.25 a week during the period of employment in one shop. Moreover, the payrolls showed that half the workers received a total of less than $99 from any single position during the year in the shops investigated.

This did not, of course, represent the total earnings from all positions during the year, a fact which could be secured only through personal interviews. Fortunately the comparatively few girls who gave us full information on this point were a thoroughly representative group in their earning capacity, as shown by the fact that the median weekly earnings for them were $9.56 as compared with median earnings of $9.69 for the much larger number whose names appeared on the payrolls. We may safely assume, therefore, that the annual earnings of the milliners whom we interviewed are a fairly accurate indication of the annual earnings of all milliners in New York City. The appalling fact disclosed is that, although the earning capacity of these girls, as represented by their median wages, was $9.56 a week, which should yield through steady work an annual income of about $500, yet the actual median annual earnings from all positions in all occupations during the year, as shown in these interviews, were but $365, or about $7.00 a week. Half the workers, it should be noted, received even less than that sum.

An income of a dollar every day in the calendar year is clearly insufficient for self-support, yet half the milliners have less than that when the wages of the busy season are spread over the long dull months. Proof of its inadequacy is merely a matter of arithmetic. One week's expenses: Board and lodging, $5.00; carfare, 60 cents; laundry, 50 cents; all other, 90 cents; total, $7.00.

Sixty cents a week for carfare is a fixed charge for most workers. Fifty cents for laundry is a low estimate. An allowance of $5.00 for lodging and food is not sufficient for health even through the most strict and continuous economy. After these three expenditures only 90 cents out of $7.00 a week remains for clothing, an important item in a wage-earning girl's equipment, and for medical care, dentistry, and contributions to relatives here or abroad. Even if 90 cents be made to stretch over these items, there is still nothing left for stamps and stationery, newspapers, vacations, recreation, church contributions, dues to club or union, insurance, or savings. Indeed, even a budget of $9.00 a week, carefully figured by the girls themselves on the basis of their own experience, could not be stretched to cover these expenditures, none of which can be regarded as unreasonable or extravagant.

This estimate is the budget of a girl living alone, but no great change need be made in the figures for the girl who lives at home. In the normal family there are usually some members who do not work for wages, so that the income of those who work is needed for more than one person. This is clearly an offset to the economies made possible by co-operative living. Moreover, many items, such as carfare, clothing, insurance, dentistry and doctors' bills, and savings, are fixed needs, whether one boards or lives at home.

This brief independent inquiry into the cost of living of milliners is confirmed in the results of the wider study in other trades made at the same time by the New York State Factory Investigating Commission. Their conclusion was that "the very lowest sum upon which a working woman can decently maintain herself in that city of the State where the rents and food prices seem about the lowest, namely, in Buffalo, is $8.20 per week the year round, and in New York City, $9.00."* Ample confirmation of this estimate can be found in the detailed report of the commission. It corroborates the estimate reached in the study of milliners.

The great outstanding fact in this investigation of the millinery trade is, then, that the career of a milliner yields less than a living wage for more than

* New York State Factory Investigating Commission, Fourth Report, 1915. Vol. I, p. 38.

half the workers, and that the most important cause of low earnings is irregular employment, due to seasonal fluctuations. This twin problem of low wages and unemployment would be serious enough if it were found only in the millinery trade. The fact that it is characteristic of nearly all of women's trades, as many investigations, official and unofficial, prove, increases its significance and its urgency a thousandfold.

The conclusion of the New York State Factory Investigating Commission, reached after exhaustive investigation and comprehensive public hearings, is clearly stated in its final report to the legislature:

> After careful deliberation and study of the results of its investigation and the testimony taken, the Commission has come to the conclusion that the State is justified in protecting the under-paid women workers and minors in the interest of the State and society. It finds that there are thousands of women and minors employed in the industries throughout the State of New York who are receiving too low a wage adequately to maintain them in health and decent comfort. The Commission believes this injuriously affects the lives and health of these underpaid workers, and that it is opposed to the best interests and welfare of the people of the State.

In order to remedy this evil, the commission recommends:

> The enactment of a law creating a Wage Commission, which, after investigation, shall establish Wage Boards, composed of representatives of employers, employes and the public, in any industry in which it has reason to believe

women and minors are receiving less than a living wage. Wherever possible, the employers and workers are to be elected by their respective groups; but if this is impossible, employers and employes shall be notified of meetings at which the work of the Wage Commission shall be explained, and the representatives of the trade asked to present recommendations to the Wage Board. The Wage Commission, after public hearings, and upon consideration of the report of the Wage Board, shall determine the amount of the living wage necessary for such women and minors, and recommend to employers payment thereof.*

The bill did not provide for compulsory enforcement. It merely empowered the commission to "recommend" to employers the payment of wages which the wage board should determine to be adequate. In this respect it followed the precedent already set in the Massachusetts law. In explanation of thus leaving the teeth out of its bill the New York Commission declared that it had made acceptance of recommendations voluntary, first, because the constitutionality of wage legislation was a question still pending in the Supreme Court of the United States, and, second, because "in an initial measure as provided in the bill recommended herewith, the question of wages should be adjusted by voluntary mutual action of those most directly concerned, aided by an enlightened public opinion. If, however, it should prove, after a fair test, that this method is ineffective, the Legislature should have unquestioned power to provide effective penalties to secure the proper

* Ibid., pp. 47–48.

enforcement of the determination of the Wage Commission."*

The application of such a measure to the millinery trade would be, then, to create a machinery for the adjustment of wages "by voluntary mutual action of those most directly concerned, aided by an enlightened public opinion." Had the bill become law in 1915 and had the wage commission thus created decided to apply it at once to the millinery trade, employers and employes would have been asked to elect representatives who, with disinterested outsiders appointed by the commission, would have formed the milliners' wage board. The duties of such a board would be to instigate "a careful investigation and after such public hearings as it finds necessary, endeavor to determine the amount of the living wage, whether by time rate or piece rate, suitable for a female employe of ordinary ability in such occupation or any or all of the branches thereof, and also suitable minimum wages for learners and apprentices and for minors below the age of eighteen years. In determining such living wage the board may take into consideration the financial condition of the industry and distribute any advance in wages that may be found necessary, to take effect at specified intervals."† With their recommendation as a basis the commission would then make its own determinations, recommending to employers the rates which they ought to pay. The only penalty for the failure of

* Ibid., p. 48.

† Ibid., p. 295.

employers to comply with these recommendations would be the publication of their names in newspapers, a measure of publicity, depending for its effectiveness upon the strength of public opinion on this subject.

Briefly, the bill would have brought together employers and employes to determine collectively what the wages should be and would have given publicity to their conclusions. We are dealing, then, not with regulation of wages by law, but with the organization of employers and employes for mutual agreement, acting with the sanction of the state. This feature of minimum wage laws, that usually they provide, not for an ultimatum by the legislature, but for investigation and conference by employers, employes and representatives of the public, is widely misunderstood. Clear understanding on this point, however, transfers the discussion from the question of whether or not it is possible to regulate wages by statute, to the much less theoretical question of whether or not the present careless, individual bargain is better than careful, official investigation, and free and frank public discussion on equal terms by the same people who now make the individual bargain without careful study, without publicity, and without equality in bargaining power.

Discussion of the theoretical aspects of such legislation or a forecast of its probable results is much less profitable than a summing up of actual experience. In Victoria, Australia, the millinery trade has been included since 1907 among the trades in which minimum rates of pay are officially determined and prescribed by wage boards established by act of government. In 1915, the chief inspector of factories in Melbourne sent us some first-hand data regarding the effects of the wage legislation.* These data are not final or conclusive as to the possible results of similar legislation in a city like New York, but they reveal certain tendencies in the trade in a community in which wages have been under public control for a period of nearly ten years.

Victoria, containing Melbourne, the largest and most important commercial city of Australasia, manufactures more millinery than any other state in the commonwealth. About 1,500 girls are employed, of whom the majority work in small shops. Of the 157 shops reported by the factory inspector, only one employed more than a hundred workers, while in 83 the force numbered less than six. As in New York state the trade includes both wholesale and retail branches, and since the seasons in these two do not coincide some milliners are able to prolong their employment by working in retail shops after the wholesale season has begun to decline.

The method of selecting the wage board is illustrated by the procedure followed in 1913 when new members were appointed, preparatory to revising

* This correspondence and statistical tables will be found in Appendix D, pp. 254–263.

the standards which had been set in 1907. The government office published notices in the newspapers asking for nominations. More names were submitted than were required. The Minister of Labor selected from the list five employers and five employes and nominated them publicly. Had one-fifth of the employers or employes in the trade objected within three weeks to any of those who had been nominated, an election would have been held conducted by the chief inspector of factories. In 1913, however, no objection was made, and the nominees were appointed by the Governor-in-Council, without an election. These ten, of whom five represented employers and five employes, nominated a chairman who was then appointed by the Governor-in-Council.

They were guided in their deliberations by the fundamental principle of wage legislation in Australia, namely, that the wage should be equal to the cost of living. As the chief inspector of factories expresses it in his letter, "The determining factor in fixing the minimum was the lowest amount upon which a girl could live in this state, if she had to keep herself." Thus it is the budget of the girl living alone which guided the wage board rather than the estimate of cost for girls living at home and partially assisted by their families. Moreover, it is not only wage rates for a single week which are considered. The inspector gives this interesting information: "The amount of lost time was also taken into consideration, and, as other trades akin to this had at that time fixed a minimum of 16s. per week of 48 hours, it was considered that, if a wage of 20s. was fixed, this would allow of some provision being made for lost time." Thus the board evidently assumed that a milliner in Victoria was out of work about 20 per cent of the year. If we were to apply the same measure to New York milliners, a girl earning a wage of $10 a week in millinery will suffer a reduction in earnings due to irregular employment during the course of the year, so that her actual weekly income, after making allowance for slack season, would be approximately $8.00. Thus, if $8.00 be the minimum standard in regular employment, the equivalent for a milliner would be $10. This is an attempt to relieve the hardship of loss of time and wages by increasing the minimum income in busy season. Finally, the inspector adds, "As the cost of living increased in the State, the minimum wage was raised to 25s. per week of 48 hours." This would indicate an assumption on the part of the wage board that the cost of living in Victoria increased 25 per cent between the two awards of 1907 and 1913.

In the award of 1913, the workers were divided into two groups; first, "all adults" who were to receive a minimum rate of 25s. per week of 48 hours, and who are called "minimum wage workers"; and second, "apprentices and improvers" whose rates of pay were specified each year for six years of employment, varying from 5s. in the first year to 20s. in the sixth, after which they received the minimum wage. Their numbers are limited in a definite ratio with reference to experienced workers, with not more than one apprentice to every three "or fraction of three" of the so-called minimum wage workers who receive the minimum rate of 25s. or higher, and not more than five improvers to every such "minimum wage worker."*

What, then, has been the effect of this regulation of wages by collective bargaining in the name of government? The inspector tells us that the number of milliners has not decreased, that the average wages have steadily advanced for the better-paid as well as for the low-wage workers, that no difficulty has been encountered in securing compliance with the awards, and that few violations have come to the attention of the factory inspectors. Do the statistics available support or modify these conclusions?

The chief inspector has sent us data which we present in four statistical tables† showing (Return

* An apprentice is defined as any person under twenty-one, bound by indentures of apprenticeship, or one who is over twenty-one and has the special sanction of the Minister of Labor to be formally apprenticed. The word "improver" is a somewhat nondescript term, covering anyone under twenty-one who is not an apprentice, not a piece worker, and not yet a regular "minimum wage worker." If over twenty-one, such a person must hold a special license from the Minister to be paid as an improver. It is in accordance with these definitions that the tables sent us from Victoria are constructed, with the group of apprentices and improvers divided in age groups from fourteen to twenty-one, and with separate figures for "minimum wage workers," and in the last four years, for piece workers as a distinct group.

† See pp. 259–261.

No. 1 A) number of women employed by ages and type of position and (Return No. 1 B) average weekly wages in each of these groups for each year from 1907 to 1914, during the operation of the law; size of millinery establishments (Return No. 2); and wages and numbers employed by ages in 1906 (Return No. 3), before the act came into effect.

Although the number employed in 1906, the year before the wage board came into existence, was 1,505, compared with 1,526 in 1914, an indication of a stationary condition, the fluctuations in intervening years were considerable, reaching a maximum of 1,810 in 1909 and a minimum of 1,364 in 1912. In the minimum year every group showed decreases. For the period as a whole, although the total remained almost the same at the end as at the beginning, the adult "minimum wage workers" and the piece workers increased, while apprentices and improvers decreased. In 1914, of every hundred workers, 36 were in the experienced group as compared with 18 in every hundred in 1907. The chief inspector of factories ascribes the decrease in juvenile employes to an amendment to the child labor law, which raised the minimum age for employment from thirteen to fifteen years except by special permission "in necessitous cases." The figures do not indicate, however, that this would account for more than a fraction of the change. Apprentices and improvers under fifteen numbered only 46 in

1907, and but seven in 1914. In both years they formed but a small proportion of the total.

Our primary interest, of course, is in the effect of the act on wages, whether it raises the underpaid to a fair standard, whether it still makes possible earnings above the minimum, or whether it has a levelling tendency. The table (Return No. 1 B, p. 260) shows clearly that for the workers as a whole the average weekly wages have increased steadily each year; that in 1914 these were 17s. 11d. as compared with 11s. 9d. in 1907, or with 10s. 10d. in 1906, the year before the law became operative. This represents an increase of 65 per cent between 1906 and 1914, with the increase between 1907, when milliners were included under the act, to 1914, amounting to 53 per cent. If each group be considered separately, instances are disclosed of decreases in average wages within that period, as in the case of apprentices and improvers fifteen years old, who averaged 3s. 5d. in 1910 and 2s. 10d. in 1911, or in the case of those seventeen years old, who averaged 5s. 5d. in 1908 and 4s. 10d. in 1909. If, however, the period as a whole be considered, each group shows increases in 1914 compared with 1907.

The gains were largest among apprentices and improvers, whose increases in average earnings in 1914 as compared with 1907 ranged from 37 per cent for the group of workers twenty-one years old to 82 per cent for those fourteen years old. The lowest rate of increase was for the "minimum wage workers" and the piece workers. As these were recorded separately from 1911 to 1914 but grouped together before 1911, it is necessary to combine them in 1914 for comparison with 1907. The average wages of minimum wage workers, including piece workers, in 1914, are thus found to be 32s. as compared with 31s. 4d. in 1907, an increase of but 2.1 per cent. Comparison of the present wages of the different groups of workers with wages in 1906 is not entirely valid because even though the workers were grouped by ages in that year, no division into apprentices, improvers, or experienced workers is shown in the table.

Small as the increase has been in the average wages of the experienced workers, however, it is noteworthy that their average earnings in 1914 were 28 per cent higher than the rate set by law. This certainly shows that it is possible to earn more than the legal minimum. On the other hand, the piece workers averaged only 20s. 1d. although it is the intent of the law that piece rates shall be so adjusted as to enable the "average worker" to earn the standard minimum wage, which was 25s. in 1914.

Has the minimum wage board been able to keep the wage standard advancing with the rising cost of living? On this point we have no adequate data, since we do not know the cost of living in Victoria. We have merely a hint which gives the basis for an illustrative discussion. We are told by the chief inspector that the wage standard was raised from 20s. to 25s. because of the increase in the cost of living. This would indicate an increase of 25 per cent in the cost of living, and earnings should have increased in that ratio if the workers were to be as well off in 1914 as in 1907. We have seen that for the group as a whole the increase was much larger than 25 per cent, but for the "minimum wage workers" it was very much less. The average milliner in this group had 8d. more in her purse in 1914 than in 1907, but she needed 7s. 10d. more with which to buy what she had had in 1907. Real wages and not merely money wages must be the measure of the worker's welfare.

For such a measure, however, exact facts regarding the purchasing power of a dollar in retail buying are essential. To discover the effects of a minimum wage law on wages we need to find out the course of money wages, and through knowledge of the changing value of a dollar, to translate money wages into real wages. Moreover, we must know what changes have taken place in processes of work affecting the wage scale, what effect rising standards have had on individual workers, whether they have been replaced by others, whether they have been subjected to increased strain in order to increase output, or whether a better standard of living and better management of shop conditions have resulted in increased efficiency, with less strain for the worker and more satisfactory production for the industry. Finally, we must begin to search for those most elusive of all facts, the effect of increased wages in an industry upon the selling price of its products, and the sum total of the effects of changes in money wages upon the entire cost of living. These are not matters of simple arithmetic, and the apparent effects or the logical forecast as to results may be wide of the mark. Higher wages may result in decreased cost of production. Higher prices following increased wages may not prove to be justified by any proportionate change in producing cost, and may result merely in enhanced profits for the entrepreneur. The fact is that on many of these vital points, conclusions are impossible because data are lacking.

The facts which we have about wages in the millinery trade in Victoria concern merely numbers employed and actual average wages for the different groups in successive years. We have no data about changes in personnel, or duration of employment of individuals. The wage data do not include range of earnings or the proportions of workers earning various specified amounts,—a more satisfactory measure than an average. As to changes in cost of living we have merely a hint. We cannot, therefore, draw definite conclusions as to the effects of wage legislation. The facts do show that the average wages in the trade as a whole have increased, that the earnings of the lowest paid workers, who must be the object of greatest concern, have shown more substantial gains than those of the highest paid, that these latter also have increased but to a less degree than the lower grades, and that the difference between the wage of the best paid and that of the lowest paid is less than before the law became effective. The average wage of adult workers is distinctly above the minimum set by law. On the whole, the workers seem to have made distinct gains while the law has been in effect. The case for wage legislation rests not alone upon such statistics as we have been able to quote but also upon the apparent satisfaction of the people of Victoria, who since the first enactment of a wage law, in 1896, have steadily increased the number of industries to which it applies.*

Perhaps the strongest argument for a wage board in the millinery trade in New York rests on the great need for concerted and intelligent action on the part of employers and employes in a trade in which at present co-operation is meager, while its problems are quite beyond the power of individuals acting alone to solve. In the first place, some irregularity of employment in the trade is undoubtedly due to inefficiency in the workers. It is an occupation attractive to many women. Frequent changes in the workrooms in the very height of the season, and the large proportion of girls whose names appeared on the payroll of any one shop a week or less give evidence of a group of drifters whose work probably was not satis-

* Webb, Sidney: Economic Theory of a Legal Minimum Wage. *Journal of Political Economy*, December, 1912.

factory to anyone. This frequent change in personnel was one of the indications of overcrowding in the trade. On the other hand, it was the testimony of the employers that highly skilled workers were scarce. Paradoxical as it may seem, these contradictory statements are simply two phases of the same general fact, that a higher standard of workmanship is desirable and that concentration of work in the hands of the more efficient would accomplish much in ridding the trade of too many casual workers.

In raising the standard of workmanship the public schools undoubtedly have a part to play. Inadequate training should be discouraged. Privately controlled commercial schools should be inspected by public educational authorities and those that do not measure up to their advertised promises should be properly disciplined. Perhaps one of the best remedies for inadequate training on a commercial basis is to offer sound training under public auspices. The movement for industrial education has reached the point where educators seek the co-operation of employers and workers. In a trade like millinery, in which the work is scattered through so many small establishments, co-operation becomes possible only when employers, on the one hand, and employes on the other, have developed some form of organization enabling them to confer regarding work problems. A wage board might offer such an opportunity.

In the second place, the attempt to agree on standards of work and wages in wage board conferences, and thus to substitute an orderly, reasonable procedure for the present chaotic individual bargain, would be likely not only to secure more adequate wages for the workers, but to lead employers to study together this important factor in their success,—the wage scale. It would help them to see that frequent changes in force, and the low grade work which is the usual accompaniment of low pay, cost too much. The impression gained by investigators in many industries is that the rush of business has precluded the employer's proper attention to labor questions, and prevented him even from studying the facts in his own shop. Many of them have no idea how much it costs to train a learner or how much might be gained for the establishment by better methods of apprenticeship; how much it costs to change experienced workers and how frequent these changes are; nor how much the workers earn in a year and what the advantage would be for the shop if fewer milliners could be kept at work during a longer season.

Most important of all the possible results of establishing wage boards would be the opportunity for groups of employers as well as employes to act together to attack the overwhelming problem of short seasons. Fashion is the chief cause of unemployment in this trade,—fashion and competition. No wage board could accomplish its purpose in this industry if it did not adjust rates with some idea of compensation for lost time in dull season. A wise board would go further and by its adjustment of rates put a premium upon regularity of employment, or a tax upon irregularity, by some such device as requiring payment of an additional sum to short-time workers. If, however, plans like this should prove inadequate in the large number of seasonal trades, some form of unemployment insurance may prove to be necessary. Whatever the plan, it would probably be successful in proportion as it brought pressure to bear to lengthen the seasons. Lengthening the seasons is going to be in part a process of skilful development of a market for slack season goods, and in part a process of co-operation by the women to whose whims we commonly attribute the evil results of changing fashions.

Women themselves will attack the problem before long. Already they are beginning to be sensitive over the revelations of the amount of unemployment due to frequent changes of style in all the many branches of the garment trades. Tentative plans are being discussed now by such important groups as the General Federation of Women's Clubs and the Consumers' League to influence the length of the seasons by educating women to new standards. Perhaps this discussion by women will help to make employers realize that the undertaking is possible and promising. At present employers are so convinced that women do not buy hats in dull season, that the most conscientious buyer finds it difficult to find any stock in hand in a millinery shop in January or August. What she finds is usually an advance model of the coming season, and if she happens to prefer to wear winter hats while winter lasts she goes away disappointed. If the employers in the trade were awake to their opportunities they could so serve women like her as to encourage rather than to discourage dull season buying.

At any rate it is a campaign worth undertaking. Perhaps the first step will be some such state action as the New York State Factory Investigating Commission had in mind when it proposed the organization of wage boards to attack two great problems not now touched by the New York labor law,—low wages and irregular employment.

SUPPLEMENTARY REPORT ON STATISTICS OF SEASONS AND WAGES

FOR the use of students especially interested in understanding the basis for conclusions in chapters IV and V, the following detailed statistics of seasons and wages are presented.

I. THE SEASONS

Facts regarding irregular employment divide naturally into two main groups, the first relating to changes in the demand for labor in the industry itself, and the second relating to the experiences of individual workers. Of the fluctuations in the industry itself, aside from changes in the personnel of the force, the payrolls told us an eloquent story. A count of the workers week by week shows the great variations in numbers employed in different months of the year. The total of wages paid each week serves also as an approximate indication of the size of the labor force. The two sets of figures are not identical, for the number of employes may remain the same, but they may work only part time and thus the wages will be less. As indicating both the income of the workers and the production of the factory, the dollar paid in wages is the most accurate unit for measuring fluctuations in employment. Table 29 shows both the numbers employed and the total wages paid each week. The diagrams on pages 72 to 75 picture the same variations.

The significance of these facts has been discussed in previous chapters. It is evident that the industry is responsible for a great waste of labor force. It is possible to estimate how great this waste is by ascertaining the total wages paid in the shops investigated in their maximum weeks, and the total wages which would have been paid in a year of fifty-two maximum weeks, and then comparing this annual, estimated wage bill with the total actually paid to milliners in these shops. Table 30 shows the result. The figures in the first column were secured by first determining the week for each establishment in which the payroll was at its maximum, and then adding together the total wages in the selected week for each shop. The figures, therefore, do not represent an amount paid out in any one week in the year, but the sum of maximum weekly outlay for wages in each of the shops whenever that maximum may have occurred.

It seems fair to conclude that the $24,000 paid in wages in the maximum weeks in all branches of the trade represents the labor capacity of the industry in these shops. At least in one week during the year each shop must purchase an amount of labor of which this figure is an index. It is not

TABLE 29.—NUMBER OF WOMEN EMPLOYED AND TOTAL WAGES PAID IN RETAIL, RETAIL-WHOLESALE, AND WHOLESALE MILLINERY ESTABLISHMENTS IN EACH WEEK OF THE YEAR 1913

Number of week	Retail		Retail-wholesale		Wholesale		All branches of trade	
	Women employed	Total wages	Women employed	Total wages	Women employed	Total wages	Women employed	Total wages
1	98	$1,002	157	$2,153	786	$6,545	1,041	$9,700
2	100	1,119	196	2,748	932	9,090	1,228	12,957
3	127	1,346	276	3,593	1,016	10,508	1,419	15,447
4	131	1,504	311	4,158	1,074	11,255	1,516	16,917
5	152	1,759	336	4,576	1,103	11,446	1,591	17,781
6	170	1,914	342	4,852	1,168	11,989	1,680	18,755
7	192	2,096	353	5,092	1,155	12,153	1,700	19,341
8	216	2,311	358	5,048	1,138	12,161	1,712	19,520
9	233	2,449	351	5,098	1,102	12,299	1,686	19,846
10	240	2,643	334	4,812	1,038	11,893	1,612	19,348
11	237	2,676	332	4,856	991	11,141	1,560	18,673
12	244	2,753	326	4,675	939	10,095	1,509	17,523
13	250	2,793	316	4,654	865	8,775	1,431	16,222
14	252	2,877	313	4,560	804	7,963	1,369	15,400
15	255	2,860	306	4,483	747	6,885	1,308	14,228
16	250	2,804	301	4,454	639	5,595	1,190	12,853
17	241	2,720	289	4,314	583	4,920	1,113	11,954
18	234	2,642	254	3,900	518	4,345	1,006	10,887
19	208	2,406	242	3,803	459	3,880	909	10,089
20	188	2,174	239	3,739	435	3,822	862	9,735
21	178	2,087	232	3,651	426	3,786	836	9,524
22	164	1,981	208	3,285	451	3,641	823	8,907
23	156	1,859	174	2,915	432	3,612	762	8,386
24	148	1,675	157	2,408	437	3,822	742	7,905
25	135	1,537	146	2,366	470	4,255	751	8,158
26	119	1,304	132	2,039	533	4,762	784	8,105
27	89	809	112	1,826	520	4,111	721	6,746
28	86	815	148	2,311	720	6,524	954	9,650
29	70	704	215	3,084	831	8,062	1,116	11,850
30	63	602	255	3,834	897	8,775	1,215	13,211
31	64	695	294	4,412	935	9,464	1,293	14,571
32	116	1,352	323	4,734	972	9,906	1,411	15,992
33	168	1,816	337	4,880	989	10,523	1,494	17,219
34	197	2,172	346	5,000	1,025	11,074	1,568	18,246
35	207	2,335	354	5,052	1,021	11,387	1,582	18,774
36	238	2,638	355	5,046	979	10,978	1,572	18,662
37	250	2,872	350	5,072	957	11,859	1,557	19,803
38	239	2,805	345	5,080	939	11,736	1,523	19,621
39	251	2,896	336	4,927	916	11,404	1,503	19,227
40	250	2,938	335	4,765	841	8,115	1,426	15,818
41	248	2,890	332	4,755	780	7,957	1,360	15,602
42	252	2,931	328	4,862	723	7,026	1,303	14,819
43	235	2,810	315	4,696	627	5,780	1,177	13,286
44	217	2,633	304	4,613	531	4,777	1,052	12,023
45	206	2,440	304	4,578	474	4,547	984	11,565
46	189	2,376	293	4,459	494	4,832	976	11,667
47	183	2,321	249	3,962	511	4,940	943	11,223
48	170	2,149	206	3,493	500	4,371	876	10,013
49	150	1,925	211	3,397	540	5,215	901	10,537
50	141	1,840	163	2,772	614	5,974	918	10,586
51	133	1,750	144	2,337	663	6,458	940	10,545
52	109	1,315	120	2,045	677	5,701	906	9,061
Average per week	181	$2,079	270	$4,004	768	$7,733	1,219	$13,830

a complete measure of the industry, of course, since it does not include all the shops in the trade. If this demand were repeated regularly throughout the year, the total wages paid by these shops would have amounted to more than a million and a quarter. The wages actually paid amounted to less than three-quarters of a million, or 57 per cent of the estimated total if there had been no seasonal variations. In other words, the trade lost 43 per cent of the labor force which it would have utilized had it been able to hold throughout the year the level attained in its busiest week.

TABLE 30.—ACTUAL ANNUAL WAGES PAID IN THE YEAR 1913, AND ESTIMATED ANNUAL WAGES FOR A YEAR OF 52 MAXIMUM WEEKS, IN 40 RETAIL, RETAIL-WHOLESALE, AND WHOLESALE MILLINERY ESTABLISHMENTS IN NEW YORK CITY [a]

Branch of trade	Total wages paid by different establishments in maximum week of year	Estimated total wages for year of 52 maximum weeks	Total actual annual wages
Retail	$3,225	$167,700	$108,120
Retail-wholesale	5,813	302,276	208,224
Wholesale	15,279	794,508	402,134
Total	$24,317	$1,264,484	$718,478

[a] Figures are for 21 wholesale, 12 retail, and seven retail-wholesale establishments.

A summary of the facts as to numbers employed and wages paid week by week (the data in Table 29) is given in Table 31, showing the maximum and minimum in each branch of the trade, the average for the year, and the per cent which the average represents of the maximum. Here the maximum is the figure for the single week of greatest employment in all the shops combined.

TABLE 31.—MAXIMUM, MINIMUM, AND AVERAGE NUMBER OF WOMEN EMPLOYED IN ANY ONE WEEK, AND MAXIMUM, MINIMUM, AND AVERAGE AMOUNT OF WAGES PAID IN ANY ONE WEEK DURING THE CALENDAR YEAR 1913, IN 40 RETAIL, RETAIL-WHOLESALE, AND WHOLESALE MILLINERY ESTABLISHMENTS[a]

	Maximum in any one week	Minimum in any one week	Average for year	Per cent average is of maximum
Women employed				
Retail . .	255	63	181	71
Retail-wholesale	358	112	270	75
Wholesale .	1,168	426	768	66
Total wages paid				
Retail . .	$2,938	$602	$2,079	71
Retail-wholesale	5,098	1,826	4,004	79
Wholesale .	12,299	3,612	7,733	63

[a] Figures are for 21 wholesale, 12 retail, and seven retail-wholesale establishments.

Thus, in the wholesale shops the average force maintained was only 66 per cent of the maximum; in retail, 71 per cent; and in retail-wholesale, 75 per cent. The figures for wages were very similar.

The differences in the figures for maximum wages in Tables 30 and 31 show a fact of significance in a discussion of unemployment statistics. In Table 31 a single week is selected in which numbers employed, or wages paid in all the shops combined, were at their maximum. In Table 30 the wages paid were noted for the maximum week in each shop and the result was obtained by adding them together for all shops, regardless of the fact that the maximum week occurred on different dates in different shops. In Table 30 the maximum wage bill is larger than in Table 31. In other words, to group the shops first and then to measure the regularity of their force and their payroll week by week tends to equalize the fluctuations actually encountered by the workers. Even in the week which is busiest for the whole group, workers may be out of employment in those establishments in which the season has taken a different course.

In all the data so far given we have been indicating merely a rough measure of variations in the industry. None of these figures can be regarded as a measure of the regularity of employment of individual workers. They must be supplemented by facts regarding individual records. The method of studying the payrolls by using a single card for each worker and copying her earnings week by week enabled us to ascertain how many weeks in the year she received pay from one shop. It did not, of course, show the length of her employment in the shop, since she may have been at work in the same place the preceding year, and may have returned in the year following the investigation.

Nor does it show her total history of employment during the year, unless she was on the payroll fifty-two weeks. Time lost in this shop may have been spent at work in another millinery establishment or in another occupation. Table 32 shows the facts as they are recorded in the individual schedules secured for 3,983 women, indicating the length of employment in one shop inthe calendar year 1913.

TABLE 32.—WEEKS THAT WOMEN WERE ON THE ANNUAL PAYROLL OF A SINGLE MILLINERY ESTABLISHMENT IN THE CALENDAR YEAR 1913, BY MAIN BRANCHES OF THE TRADE

Number of weeks [a]	Women on payroll of a single establishment the specified number of weeks			All women		
	Retail shops	Retail-wholesale shops	Wholesale shops	Number	Per cent	
1	78	95	607	780	19.6	
2	37	41	307	385	9.7	40.1
3	21	29	196	246	6.2	
4	17	17	148	182	4.6	
5	14	16	128	158	4.0	
6	16	9	104	129	3.2	
7	17	10	74	101	2.5	11.9
8	12	16	59	87	2.2	
9	8	8	57	73	1.8	
10	15	8	53	76	1.9	
11	16	13	56	85	2.1	7.7
12	16	11	49	76	1.9	
13	11	8	44	63	1.6	
14	13	15	36	64	1.6	
15	6	12	32	50	1.3	5.8
16	3	10	37	50	1.3	

[a] The number of weeks in this table is based on the number of times the worker's name appeared on the payroll of a shop, and in this way a fraction of a week is in some cases counted as a week. For example, if a milliner began work in a given establishment on Wednesday of one week, and worked there for the following three weeks, leaving on a Wednesday three weeks after she started, her length of employment would be counted as four weeks, that is, four payroll periods.

TABLE 32.—(*Continued*)

Number of weeks	Women on payroll of a single establishment the specified number of weeks			All women		
	Retail shops	Retail-wholesale shops	Wholesale shops	Number	Per cent	
17	2	14	40	56	1.4	
18	10	6	22	38	.9	
19	6	8	35	49	1.2	4.2
20	2	5	22	29	.7	
21	2	6	19	27	.7	
22	1	4	29	34	.8	
23	1	6	20	27	.7	3.0
24	2	6	22	30	.8	
25	6	4	16	26	.6	
26	3	4	28	35	.9	2.5
27	3	4	10	17	.4	
28	5	6	15	26	.6	
29	3	3	15	21	.5	
30	4	3	22	29	.7	
31	2	6	21	29	.7	2.3
32	3	6	8	17	.4	
33	8	3	24	35	.9	
34	6	7	6	19	.5	
35	8	6	14	28	.7	3.0
36	3	16	17	36	.9	
37	5	4	23	32	.8	
38	7	8	15	30	.8	
39	9	6	21	36	.9	3.5
40	6	9	25	40	1.0	
41	5	11	20	36	.9	
42	6	13	19	38	1.0	
43	4	18	9	31	.8	3.7
44	7	12	21	40	1.0	
45	8	15	17	40	1.0	
46	14	18	20	52	1.3	
47	13	9	20	42	1.1	4.7
48	2	22	27	51	1.3	
49	6	22	37	65	1.6	
50	7	20	43	70	1.8	
51	15	8	34	57	1.4	7.6
52	8	5	97	110	2.8	
Total	502	641	2,840	3,983	100.0	
Median number of weeks[b]	11	17	6	8		

[b] This is a designation of the median group, not an exact median worked out by formula. (See footnote b, p. 83.)

II. WAGES

The various types of wage statistics secured are described in Chapter V. All the tables showing rates of pay as distinct from earnings, and several of those dealing with earnings, are presented in this supplementary report. Piece workers are omitted, of course, from tables dealing with wage rates, since these tables apply only to workers paid by the week. Table 33 shows the wage rates recorded for the week workers on the current payroll; that is to say, the data for the single payroll period nearest the date of investigation in each shop. To simplify the presentation the shops are classified as retail and wholesale, including with the retail establishments those separated in some previous tables as retail-wholesale. In type of workmanship, these shops are part of the retail group, although the fact that they have some wholesale trade does affect their seasons and therefore made it desirable to keep them separate in Chapter IV.

In retail, 148, or 27 per cent, were rated at less than $8.00 a week, and in wholesale the number was 208, or 23 per cent. For the whole group of week workers the median wage rate was $10.77. The median in retail was higher than for week workers in wholesale. It should be remembered, however, that these figures take no account of the piece workers in wholesale. Table 34 shows the actual earnings of the same group of workers with the addition of those paid by the piece.

TABLE 33.—WEEKLY RATES OF WAGES FOR WOMEN WEEK WORKERS EMPLOYED IN RETAIL AND WHOLESALE MILLINERY ESTABLISHMENTS, AS SHOWN BY CURRENT PAYROLL. 1914

Weekly rate of wages	Women employed in		All women	
	Retail shops	Wholesale shops	Number	Per cent
Less than $2	4	..	4	.3
$2 and less than $3	18	4	22	1.5
$3 and less than $4	25	12	37	2.6
$4 and less than $5	21	24	45	3.1
$5 and less than $6	26	38	64	4.4
$6 and less than $7	21	58	79	5.5
$7 and less than $8	33	72	105	7.3
$8 and less than $9	37	100	137	9.5
$9 and less than $10	33	95	128	8.8
$10 and less than $12	52	145	197	13.6
$12 and less than $14	92	167	259	17.9
$14 and less than $16	78	91	169	11.7
$16 and less than $18	24	14	38	2.6
$18 and less than $20	10	18	28	1.9
$20 and less than $25	19	17	36	2.5
$25 and less than $30	14	19	33	2.3
$30 and less than $35	8	11	19	1.3
$35 and less than $40	6	7	13	.9
$40 or more	25	9	34	2.3
Total	546	901	1,447[a]	100.0
Median wage rate[b]	$12.04	$10.51	$10.77	

[a] Of the 1,951 women whose names appeared on the current payroll, 504 were piece workers in wholesale shops whose rates of pay could not be ascertained, since they are determined by unit of production rather than by unit of time worked.

[b] See footnote b, p. 83, and footnote a, p. 139.

The median earnings actually received by workers in retail, all of whom were week workers, was $10.90, while the median rate for the same group was $12.04. Of the whole number, 35 per cent

TABLE 34.—ACTUAL EARNINGS DURING ONE WEEK FOR WOMEN PIECE AND WEEK WORKERS EMPLOYED IN RETAIL AND WHOLESALE MILLINERY ESTABLISHMENTS, AS SHOWN BY CURRENT PAY-ROLL. 1914

Weekly earnings	Women employed in		All women	
	Retail shops	Wholesale shops	Number	Per cent
Less than $2	8	41	49	2.6
$2 and less than $3	26	35	61	3.3
$3 and less than $4	28	42	70	3.7
$4 and less than $5	23	66	89	4.8
$5 and less than $6	31	85	116	6.2
$6 and less than $7	25	93	118	6.3
$7 and less than $8	38	107	145	7.8
$8 and less than $9	35	140	175	9.4
$9 and less than $10	32	129	161	8.6
$10 and less than $12	50	222	272	14.5
$12 and less than $14	84	171	255	13.6
$14 and less than $16	65	80	145	7.8
$16 and less than $18	24	25	49	3.9
$18 and less than $20	9	15	24	
$20 and less than $25	16	28	44	4.1
$25 and less than $30	15	18	33	
$30 and less than $35	8	10	18	1.7
$35 and less than $40	7	7	14	
$40 or more	22	9	31	1.7
Total	546	1,323	1,869[a]	100.0
Median earnings[b]	$10.90	$9.41	$9.69	

[a] Of the 1,951 women whose names appeared on the current pay-roll, 82 were piece workers whose earnings were not included as they had been employed only five days during the week on account of a legal holiday, and their earnings were not strictly comparable with those in shops having a normal six-day working week.

[b] See footnote b, p. 83, and footnote a, p. 139.

earned less than $8.00. The table shows also that the range of earnings is wide, varying from less

TABLE 35.—WEEKLY RATES OF WAGES, BY YEARS IN THE TRADE, FOR WOMEN WEEK WORKERS EMPLOYED IN MILLINERY ESTABLISHMENTS, AS SHOWN BY CURRENT PAYROLL. 1914

Weekly rate of wages	Women employed in the trade									All women
	Less than 1 year	1 year and less than 2	2 years and less than 3	3 years and less than 5	5 years and less than 7	7 years and less than 10	10 years and less than 15	15 years and less than 20	20 years or more	
Less than $2	4	..	..	..	..	..	..	..	..	4
$2 and less than $3	15	1	..	..	..	..	..	..	..	16
$3 and less than $4	22	7	..	..	..	..	..	..	..	29
$4 and less than $5	16	9	6	1	..	..	..	..	..	32
$5 and less than $6	10	14	14	4	2	..	..	..	..	44
$6 and less than $7	6	12	23	12	..	..	..	..	..	53
$7 and less than $8	7	11	20	34	10	..	..	..	..	82
$8 and less than $9	3	6	12	56	14	7	4	..	..	102
$9 and less than $10	..	2	6	40	19	9	4	..	..	80
$10 and less than $12	1	1	5	45	44	20	11	4	..	131
$12 and less than $14	1	..	2	18	48	78	31	5	5	188
$14 and less than $16	..	..	..	1	20	47	50	5	6	129
$16 and less than $18	..	..	..	1	4	8	12	3	2	30
$18 and less than $20	..	..	..	..	1	5	8	1	2	17
$20 and less than $25	..	..	..	..	1	2	15	5	3	26
$25 and less than $30	..	..	..	1	3	4	3	4	..	15
$30 and less than $35	..	..	..	..	..	2	8	3	2	15
$35 and less than $40	..	..	..	..	..	2	4	3	1	10
$40 or more	..	..	..	..	..	2	9	8	4	23
Total	85	63	88	213	166	186	159	41	25	1,026[a]
Median wage rate[b]	$4.09	$6.04	$7.05	$8.99	$11.54	$13.13	$15.24	$22.50	$17.50	$10.82

[a] Of the 1,951 women whose names appeared on the current payroll, 588 did not answer the questions called for on the personal record (Card D). Of the remainder (1,363), 331 were piece workers and six did not state years in the trade.

[b] See footnote b, p. 83, and footnote a, p. 139.

than $2.00 to more than $40, with 11 per cent earning $16 or more.

Table 35 shows the rates of wages of week workers and Tables 36 A and 36 B show the earnings, classified according to length of experience, for both week and piece workers. The number considered is less than in the tables giving rates and earnings because the latter represented payroll transcriptions, while the tables which follow are based on the cards filled by the girls in the workrooms. As already explained, not all of those listed on the current payroll filled these cards.

Table 35, showing weekly rates, brings out some interesting facts. None of those getting less than $4.00 had had as much as two years' experience. Only 14 of the 766 getting $8.00 or more had had less than two years' experience. Table 36, showing actual earnings in a given week, reveals low earnings for some workers of long experience, doubtless because of the presence of other factors, such as fines for tardiness and loss of days through illnes s or other causes. On the whole, there is a steady increase with experience.

If experience be a factor in wages, it follows naturally that wages will vary for different age groups, although the two sets of figures will not be identical for the reason that milliners have begun work at different ages. A woman of twenty years' experience may have begun work at fourteen or at twenty, or one who has been a milliner three years may be seventeen or thirty-five. Moreover,

TABLE 36A.—ACTUAL EARNINGS DURING ONE WEEK, BY YEARS IN THE TRADE, FOR WOMEN WEEK WORKERS EMPLOYED IN MILLINERY ESTABLISHMENTS, AS SHOWN BY CURRENT PAYROLL. 1914

Weekly earnings	Women employed in the trade									All women
	Less than 1 year	1 year and less than 2	2 years and less than 3	3 years and less than 5	5 years and less than 7	7 years and less than 10	10 years and less than 15	15 years and less than 20	20 years or more	
Less than $2	7	1	..	1	..	..	..	..	..	9
$2 and less than $3	21	..	3	1	..	1	..	..	..	26
$3 and less than $4	16	11	1	1	..	1	1	..	..	31
$4 and less than $5	15	8	5	1	..	1	..	..	..	30
$5 and less than $6	9	15	23	12	2	2	..	..	..	63
$6 and less than $7	8	12	22	13	2	2	..	..	..	59
$7 and less than $8	4	11	14	42	11	2	3	2	..	89
$8 and less than $9	2	2	10	55	18	9	6	1	..	103
$9 and less than $10	1	2	4	30	22	12	3	..	..	74
$10 and less than $12	1	1	5	40	40	33	15	2	..	137
$12 and less than $14	1	..	1	14	45	61	37	4	7	170
$14 and less than $16	..	..	..	1	18	37	39	6	5	106
$16 and less than $18	..	..	..	1	4	8	10	2	1	26
$18 and less than $20	..	..	..	..	..	6	7	1	2	16
$20 and less than $25	..	..	..	..	1	1	14	5	3	24
$25 and less than $30	..	..	..	1	3	4	4	4	..	16
$30 and less than $35	..	..	..	..	..	2	8	3	2	15
$35 and less than $40	..	..	..	..	..	2	4	4	1	11
$40 or more	..	..	..	..	..	2	8	7	4	21
Total	85	63	88	213	166	186	159	41	25	1,026[a]
Median earnings[b]	$3.91	$5.77	$6.55	$8.65	$11.14	$12.70	$14.81	$22.50	$17.00	$10.33

[a] Of the 1,951 women whose names appeared on the current payroll, 588 did not answer the questions called for on the personal record (Card D). Of the remainder (1,363), 331 were piece workers and six did not state years in the trade.

[b] See footnote b, p. 83, and footnote a, p. 139.

TABLE 36B.—ACTUAL EARNINGS DURING ONE WEEK, BY YEARS IN THE TRADE, FOR WOMEN PIECE WORKERS EMPLOYED IN MILLINERY ESTABLISHMENTS, AS SHOWN BY CURRENT PAYROLL. 1914

Weekly earnings	Women employed in the trade									All women
	Less than 1 year	1 year and less than 2	2 years and less than 3	3 years and less than 5	5 years and less than 7	7 years and less than 10	10 years and less than 15	15 years and less than 20	20 years or more	
Less than $2	..	1	1	1	1	..	1	..	..	5
$2 and less than $3	..	3	..	2	..	1	..	1	..	7
$3 and less than $4	..	..	1	3	..	2	..	..	1	7
$4 and less than $5	..	1	1	1	1	3	4	1	..	12
$5 and less than $6	..	1	1	5	2	4	3	..	3	19
$6 and less than $7	..	..	5	4	2	4	3	..	3	21
$7 and less than $8	..	1	1	3	2	6	2	1	..	16
$8 and less than $9	..	..	3	7	6	4	5	2	1	28
$9 and less than $10	..	..	5	8	3	8	7	1	2	34
$10 and less than $12	..	1	3	7	18	11	8	3	..	51
$12 and less than $14	..	1	..	5	3	3	7	3	1	23
$14 and less than $16	..	..	..	1	1	1	1	2	2	8
$16 and less than $18	..	..	..	..	..	2	2	..	1	5
$18 and less than $20	..	..	..	1	..	..	..	..	..	1
$20 and less than $25	..	..	..	..	2	..	1	1	1	5
$25 and less than $30	..	..	..	1	..	..	..	..	..	1
$30 or more	..	..	..	..	..	..	..	..	1	1
Total	..	9	21	49	41	49	44	15	16	244[a]
Median earnings[b]	..	$4.50	$8.17	$8.79	$10.39	$9.06	$9.57	$11.25	$9.00	$9.21

[a] Of the 331 piece workers whose names appeared on the current payroll, and who filled out the personal record (card D), 82 had been employed only five days during the week on account of a legal holiday and five did not state years in the trade.

[b] See footnote b, p. 83, and footnote a, p. 139.

a given wage has a different meaning for the girl of seventeen and the woman of thirty-five. Tables 37 and 38 show rates and earnings in the different age groups.

Except in the higher age groups in which the numbers are too few to warrant conclusions, the median wage in both tables steadily increases with age. In Table 38, as in preceding tables, median earnings are almost invariably lower than rates for the same groups. Table 37, giving wage rates, shows that of the 125 receiving less than $6.00, 83 were under eighteen and 42 were eighteen or older. In every age group except the last, however, a wage of less than $10 is received by someone. In Table 38, showing earnings, we discover that of the 507 girls under twenty-one, only two received $16 or more; but, on the other hand, of the 180 women of thirty years or older, as many as 113 received less than $16. The higher wages are not attained by more than a small proportion of the workers and then only by the more mature. That the prizes are chiefly reserved for those who have the ability to become designers or forewomen is shown in Tables 39 and 40, giving rates and earnings according to positions held. The numbers treated here are identical with those for whom current payroll statistics were copied, since the facts about the occupation of each worker were secured from the employer and did not depend upon the workers' replies.

TABLE 37.—WEEKLY RATES OF WAGES, BY AGES, FOR WOMEN WEEK WORKERS EMPLOYED IN MILLINERY ESTABLISHMENTS, AS SHOWN BY CURRENT PAYROLL. 1914

Weekly rate of wages	Women									All women
	14 years and less than 16	16 years and less than 18	18 years and less than 21	21 years and less than 25	25 years and less than 30	30 years and less than 35	35 years and less than 40	40 years and less than 45	45 years or more	
Less than $2	..	2	2	..	..	..	..	..	..	4
$2 and less than $3	2	9	5	..	..	..	..	..	..	16
$3 and less than $4	4	19	5	1	..	..	..	..	..	29
$4 and less than $5	7	18	6	1	..	..	..	..	..	32
$5 and less than $6	3	19	19	3	..	..	..	..	..	44
$6 and less than $7	..	28	21	4	..	..	..	..	..	53
$7 and less than $8	..	19	44	14	2	..	2	1	..	82
$8 and less than $9	..	13	55	24	8	2	..	..	..	102
$9 and less than $10	..	4	48	22	4	1	1	..	..	80
$10 and less than $12	..	2	52	53	13	8	5	..	..	133
$12 and less than $14	..	..	22	98	52	10	1	3	2	188
$14 and less than $16	..	..	8	50	54	8	3	4	2	129
$16 and less than $18	..	..	..	10	10	6	2	1	..	29
$18 and less than $20	..	..	..	3	8	2	3	1	..	17
$20 and less than $25	..	..	..	3	10	8	4	..	1	26
$25 and less than $30	..	..	1	4	6	3	1	..	..	15
$30 and less than $35	..	..	..	1	7	5	1	..	1	15
$35 and less than $40	..	..	..	1	2	6	1	..	..	10
$40 or more	..	..	..	2	4	8	6	1	2	23
Total	16	133	288	294	180	67	30	11	8	1,027[a]
Median wage rate[b]	$4.14	$5.94	$8.76	$12.40	$14.39	$17.50	$18.67	$15.17	$20.00	$10.81

[a] Of the 1,363 women for whom workers' reports were secured, 331 were piece workers, and five of the week workers did not state age.

[b] See footnote b, p. 83, and footnote a, p. 139.

TABLE 38.—ACTUAL EARNINGS DURING ONE WEEK, BY AGES, FOR WOMEN PIECE AND WEEK WORKERS EMPLOYED IN MILLINERY ESTABLISHMENTS, AS SHOWN BY CURRENT PAYROLL. 1914

Weekly earnings	Women									All women
	14 years and less than 16	16 years and less than 18	18 years and less than 21	21 years and less than 25	25 years and less than 30	30 years and less than 35	35 years and less than 40	40 years and less than 45	45 years or more	
Less than $2	1	4	5	2	1	1	..	..	..	14
$2 and less than $3	3	15	10	4	..	1	..	1	..	34
$3 and less than $4	4	20	7	4	3	..	..	..	1	39
$4 and less than $5	6	14	9	4	4	2	2	..	1	42
$5 and less than $6	2	20	32	16	7	2	2	1	1	83
$6 and less than $7	..	33	30	7	6	..	1	2	2	81
$7 and less than $8	..	18	48	22	9	1	4	2	1	105
$8 and less than $9	..	13	62	33	11	7	1	3	1	131
$9 and less than $10	..	6	46	35	11	7	1	..	2	108
$10 and less than $12	..	2	64	74	34	5	7	3	..	189
$12 and less than $14	..	..	23	90	52	19	3	4	2	193
$14 and less than $16	..	..	8	42	44	8	5	5	2	114
$16 and less than $18	..	..	..	10	11	5	3	1	..	30
$18 and less than $20	..	..	..	5	6	3	2	1	..	17
$20 and less than $25	..	..	..	3	10	9	4	..	3	29
$25 and less than $30	..	..	2	4	6	4	1	..	..	17
$30 and less than $35	..	..	..	1	7	5	1	..	1	15
$35 and less than $40	..	..	..	1	2	..	7	2	..	12
$40 or more	..	..	..	2	4	6	6	1	2	21
Total	16	145	346	359	228	85	50	26	19	1,274[a]
Median earnings[b]	$4.00	$5.98	$8.52	$11.26	$12.97	$13.69	$15.00	$12.25	$12.25	$10.00

[a] Of the 1,363 women for whom workers' reports were secured, seven did not state age and 82 were piece workers whose earnings were not included as they had been employed only five days during the week on account of a legal holiday.

[b] See footnote b, p. 83, and footnote a, p. 139.

TABLE 39.—WEEKLY RATES OF WAGES, BY OCCUPATIONS, FOR WOMEN WEEK WORKERS EMPLOYED IN MILLINERY ESTABLISHMENTS, AS SHOWN BY CURRENT PAYROLL.

1914

Weekly rate of wages	Women employed as														All women
	Forewomen and assistants	Designers	Trimmers	Copyists	Makers	Preparers	Improvers	Apprentices	Floor workers	Machine operators	Crimpers, cutters, and wire-frame makers	Flower and feather makers	Straw[a] and crown sewers	All other manufacturing occupations	
Less than $2 . .	..	..	..	..	..	..	..	4	..	..	..	..	..	..	4
$2 and less than $3	..	..	..	..	..	..	2	20	..	..	..	..	..	..	22
$3 and less than $4	..	..	..	..	..	1	5	30	1	..	..	..	..	..	37
$4 and less than $5	..	..	..	..	2	4	9	21	7	..	1	1	..	..	45
$5 and less than $6	..	..	..	..	1	9	16	18	11	..	7	1	..	1	64
$6 and less than $7	..	..	..	1	5	34	25	2	9	1	1	..	1	..	79
$7 and less than $8	..	..	..	1	19	48	13	1	13	4	1	3	1	1	105
$8 and less than $9	..	..	..	9	27	82	6	1	6	5	..	..	..	1	137
$9 and less than $10	2	..	1	15	27	61	2	..	7	4	3	5	1	..	128
$10 and less than $12	2	..	9	58	61	33	..	..	7	14	7	4	1	1	197
$12 and less than $14	2	..	24	104	92	14	..	..	11	7	4	..	1	..	259
$14 and less than $16	3	3	16	59	67	1	..	..	3	11	3	2	..	1	169
$16 and less than $18	2	..	7	9	16	..	..	..	1	..	..	3	..	..	38
$18 and less than $20	4	4	1	9	5	..	..	..	..	3	1	1	..	..	28
$20 and less than $25	5	5	4	8	7	..	..	..	2	..	1	4	..	..	36
$25 and less than $30	10	12	5	3	..	..	..	..	1	1	..	1	..	..	33
$30 and less than $35	5	8	2	2	..	..	..	..	..	..	1	1	..	..	19
$35 and less than $40	2	9	1	1	..	..	..	..	..	..	..	..	..	..	13
$40 or more . .	2	31	..	..	..	..	..	..	..	..	..	1	..	..	34
Total . .	39	72	70	279	329	287	78	97	79	50	30	27	5	5	1,447[b]
Median wage rate[c].	$24.50	$37.22	$14.13	$13.07	$12.49	$8.58	$6.28	$3.49	$7.63	$11.00	$10.50	$11.75	$9.50	$8.50	$10.77

[a] Only one straw sewer was paid on a time basis.

[b] Of the 1,951 women whose names appeared on the current payroll, 504 were piece workers whose rates of pay were not ascertainable. Of these piece workers, 22 were machine operators, four were crimpers, cutters and wire-frame makers, 11 straw and crown sewers, 457 copyists, seven trimmers, two preparers, and one a maker.

[c] See footnote b, p. 83, and footnote a, p. 139.

TABLE 40.—ACTUAL EARNINGS DURING ONE WEEK, BY OCCUPATIONS, FOR WOMEN PIECE AND WEEK WORKERS EMPLOYED IN MILLINERY ESTABLISHMENTS, AS SHOWN BY CURRENT PAYROLL. 1914

Weekly earnings	Women employed as														All women
	Forewomen and assistants	Designers	Trimmers	Copyists	Makers	Preparers	Improvers	Apprentices	Floor workers	Machine operators	Crimpers, cutters, and wire-frame makers	Flower and feather makers	Straw[a] and crown sewers	All other manufacturing occupations	
Less than $2	..	..	..	27	1	7	1	10	2	1	..	..	..	..	49
$2 and less than $3	..	..	..	19	6	8	2	23	2	..	..	..	1	..	61
$3 and less than $4	..	1	1	19	5	8	9	27	..	..	..	..	..	..	70
$4 and less than $5	..	1	2	28	6	10	6	22	8	..	1	1	3	1	89
$5 and less than $6	..	..	1	30	4	29	22	12	7	1	7	1	1	1	116
$6 and less than $7	..	1	4	29	4	38	24	2	10	2	2	..	2	..	118
$7 and less than $8	..	..	1	33	29	51	9	..	12	4	1	3	2	..	145
$8 and less than $9	..	..	5	61	28	64	4	1	6	3	1	1	..	1	175
$9 and less than $10	2	..	5	66	27	42	1	..	7	2	2	6	1	..	161
$10 and less than $12	2	..	12	145	58	20	..	..	8	16	7	2	1	1	272
$12 and less than $14	2	1	19	116	83	11	..	..	10	7	3	2	1	..	255
$14 and less than $16	3	3	10	57	52	1	..	..	3	12	3	1	..	1	146
$16 and less than $18	2	..	5	19	16	..	..	..	1	..	..	3	2[a]	..	48
$18 and less than $20	4	4	1	6	4	..	..	..	..	3	1	1	..	..	24
$20 and less than $25	5	8	3	13	7	..	..	..	2	1	1	4	..	..	44
$25 and less than $30	10	10	5	4	..	..	..	..	1	2	..	..	1[a]	..	33
$30 and less than $35	5	6	2	2	..	..	..	..	..	1	1	1	..	..	18
$35 and less than $40	2	9	1	1	..	..	..	..	..	..	..	..	1[a]	..	14
$40 or more	2	28	..	..	..	..	..	..	..	..	..	1	..	..	31
Total	39	72	77	675	330	289	78	97	79	55	30	27	16	5	1,869[b]
Median earnings[c]	$24.50	$35.56	$12.79	$10.35	$11.90	$7.87	$5.95	$3.39	$7.63	$11.50	$10.25	$11.75	$7.25	$8.50	$9.69

[a] Of the five straw sewers whose names appeared on the current payroll, four were piece workers making high earnings. They are designated in this column with an *a*. (See note on straw sewers, Appendix B, pp. 248–249.)

[b] Of the 1,951 women whose names appeared on the current payroll, 82 were piece workers whose earnings were not included as they had been employed only five days during the week on account of a legal holiday.

[c] See footnote b, p. 83, and footnote a, p. 139.

The column for machine operators includes those who prepare various parts of the trimming on machine, but not the straw sewers, who are separately recorded.* The table of rates shows only three of the 72 designers receiving less than $18 a week. Of the 97 apprentices, four were earning $6.00 or more. The median rate for milliners, excluding forewomen and their assistants, designers, and apprentices, was $10.88, and the median actual earnings $9.63.

Closely related to the data regarding length of experience in the trade are the statistics of the duration of employment in one establishment in relation to wages, as shown in Table 41.

The steady increase in median earnings with increasing duration of employment in one establishment seems to indicate that it pays to stay as long as possible in one shop. The increase is rather surprising, as the prevalent impression that changes from shop to shop result advantageously in wages would not have led one to suppose that the length of experience in one establishment would have been shown to be so distinct a factor in increased pay. Of course the comparatively high median for those employed less than one year in the shop does indicate that many in this group have had experience in other shops. It should be noted that the group numbers 421, of whom only 85, as already pointed out in an earlier chapter,† have

* See Appendix B, p. 248, for note on wages in straw sewing.

† See Table 11, p. 85.

TABLE 41.—ACTUAL EARNINGS DURING ONE WEEK, BY YEARS IN THE PRESENT ESTABLISHMENT, FOR WOMEN PIECE AND WEEK WORKERS EMPLOYED IN MILLINERY ESTABLISHMENTS, AS SHOWN BY CURRENT PAYROLL. 1914

Weekly earnings	Women employed in present establishment													All women
	Less than 1 year	1 year and less than 2	2 years and less than 3	3 years and less than 4	4 years and less than 5	5 years and less than 6	6 years and less than 7	7 years and less than 8	8 years and less than 9	9 years and less than 10	10 years and less than 15	15 years and less than 20	20 years or more	
Less than $2 . . .	11	2	..	..	1	..	..	..	..	..	..	..	..	14
$2 and less than $3	32	1	..	..	..	1	..	..	..	..	..	..	..	34
$3 and less than $4	23	12	1	2	1	..	..	..	..	..	..	..	..	39
$4 and less than $5	24	11	3	1	1	..	1	..	..	1	..	..	..	42
$5 and less than $6	42	13	23	1	..	2	..	1	1	..	..	..	..	83
$6 and less than $7	40	15	12	8	1	1	1	..	2	..	1	..	..	81
$7 and less than $8	40	26	9	15	7	2	1	1	1	..	2	1	..	105
$8 and less than $9	40	29	18	16	12	5	3	2	1	..	5	..	..	131
$9 and less than $10	32	22	13	13	12	7	4	1	..	..	4	..	..	108
$10 and less than $12	49	32	20	20	25	13	9	7	8	1	5	1	..	190
$12 and less than $14	47	28	21	21	23	13	8	9	6	4	13	1	..	194
$14 and less than $16	13	5	8	16	18	9	11	7	6	7	11	3	..	114
$16 and less than $18	4	5	1	4	4	2	3	2	..	2	4	..	1	32
$18 and less than $20	6	1	1	2	1	1	..	..	1	..	3	..	..	16
$20 and less than $25	2	1	3	1	2	3	1	1	3	..	11	..	2	30
$25 and less than $30	4	..	2	1	..	2	2	1	..	2	1	2	..	17
$30 and less than $35	5	2	2	1	1	..	..	..	2	1	..	1	..	15
$35 and less than $40	3	1	1	1	2	..	1	..	1	..	1	1	..	12
$40 or more . .	4	3	5	..	1	..	..	2	..	..	4	1	1	21
Total . . .	421	209	143	123	112	61	45	34	32	18	65	11	4	1,278[a]
Median earnings[b] .	$7.96	$8.84	$9.42	$10.55	$11.43	$11.92	$12.70	$13.20	$13.25	$15.00	$14.42	$14.83	$22.50	$10.02

[a] Of the 1,363 women for whom workers' reports were secured, 82 were piece workers whose earnings were not included as they had been employed only five days during the week on account of a legal holiday; and of the remaining 1,281 women, 3 did not state years in the present establishment.

[b] See footnote b, p. 83, and footnote a, p. 139.

been milliners less than a year. About one in five, 21 per cent, had worked five years or longer in the same shop.

The data so far quoted all relate to the current payroll for one week. In presenting the statistics drawn from the annual payroll we have not selected one typical week, but have ascertained the total earnings of each worker and then divided this sum by the number of times her name was on the payroll, thus determining the average contents of weekly pay envelopes throughout the year. These averages for the whole group have been discussed in Chapter V. Table 42, following, shows the average weekly earnings in different occupational groups.

The most noteworthy feature of the table is the fact that the median earnings are lower in all but one of the corresponding groups than were shown in Table 40, which gave the actual earnings during one week. The difference was probably due chiefly to the losses in working time during the longer period covered by these statistics.

Whether or not there is any relation between the ability of a worker as measured by her earnings and the number of weeks she is employed in one shop in a year, can best be shown by a study of the wage distribution according to the duration of employment, as in Table 43.

In a thoroughly regularized industry, and one in which the force was stable, only so many jobs would terminate within the year as might repre-

TABLE 42.—AVERAGE WEEKLY EARNINGS DURING PERIOD OF EMPLOYMENT, BY OCCUPATIONS, FOR WOMEN EMPLOYED IN ANY ONE MILLINERY ESTABLISHMENT FOR MORE THAN ONE WEEK IN THE CALENDAR YEAR 1913

Average weekly earnings	Women employed as												All women
	Forewomen	Designers	Trimmers	Copyists	Makers	Preparers	Improvers	Apprentices	Floor workers	Machine operators	Straw and crown sewers	Employes in all other manufacturing occupations	
Less than $3	..	..	1	40	7	11	7	150	10	5	1	2	234
$3 and less than $4	..	..	..	41	5	20	27	57	14	2	1	1	168
$4 and less than $5	..	..	1	73	11	65	32	27	15	6	3	11	244
$5 and less than $6	..	..	4	86	22	88	37	11	15	7	3	11	284
$6 and less than $7	..	..	7	119	42	105	24	1	8	5	4	4	319
$7 and less than $8	..	1	4	116	48	65	8	1	9	19	6	7	284
$8 and less than $10	2	1	28	271	126	57	2	..	15	33	9	20	564
$10 and less than $12	5	1	39	246	130	9	..	..	14	28	5	5	482
$12 and less than $15	7	5	25	119	125	4	..	..	11	19	9	10	334
$15 and less than $20	9	10	12	51	33	..	..	..	6	5	9	8	143
$20 and less than $25	6	19	5	7	2	..	..	..	1	1	7	3	51
$25 and less than $35	6	21	8	5	..	..	..	..	..	1	3	2	46
$35 and less than $50	4	21	2	..	..	..	..	..	..	1	..	1	29
$50 or more	1	20	..	..	..	..	..	..	..	..	..	..	21
Total	40	99	136	1,174	551	424	137	247	118	132	60	85	3,203[a]
Median average earnings[b]	$18.50	$30.75	$11.06	$8.88	$10.25	$6.27	$5.13	$2.52	$6.42	$9.31	$11.00	$8.59	$8.25

[a] Of the 3,983 women whose names appeared on the annual payroll at any time during the year, 780 were on the payroll a week or less in the calendar year and were omitted from this table.

[b] See footnote b, p. 83, and footnote a, p. 139.

TABLE 43.—AVERAGE WEEKLY EARNINGS DURING PERIOD OF EMPLOYMENT, BY NUMBER OF WEEKS ON THE PAYROLL DURING THIS PERIOD, FOR WOMEN EMPLOYED IN ANY ONE MILLINERY ESTABLISHMENT FOR MORE THAN ONE WEEK IN THE CALENDAR YEAR 1913

Average weekly earnings	Women employed in any one establishment in the calendar year 1913			All women
	More than 1 week and less than 10	10 weeks and less than 20	20 weeks or more[a]	
Less than $2	62	18	1	81
$2 and less than $3	105	27	21	153
$3 and less than $4	105	24	39	168
$4 and less than $5	157	37	50	244
$5 and less than $6	160	56	68	284
$6 and less than $7	167	64	88	319
$7 and less than $8	121	52	111	284
$8 and less than $9	117	45	109	271
$9 and less than $10	93	55	145	293
$10 and less than $12	133	114	235	482
$12 and less than $14	58	40	150	248
$14 and less than $16	28	25	78	131
$16 and less than $18	11	12	22	45
$18 and less than $20	12	16	25	53
$20 and less than $25	18	8	25	51
$25 and less than $30	5	5	16	26
$30 and less than $35	2	5	13	20
$35 and less than $40	1	1	16	18
$40 or more	6	3	23	32
Total	1,361	607	1,235	3,203[b]
Median average earnings[c]	$6.52	$8.57	$9.90	$8.25

[a] The group on the payroll 20 weeks or longer represents for the most part the permanent portion of the force. Of the 1,235 in this group, 78 per cent remained 30 weeks or more, and more than half (54.4 per cent) remained 40 weeks or more, while only 22 per cent stayed less than 30 weeks.

[b] Of the 3,983 women who appeared on the annual payroll at any time during the year, 780 were on the payroll a week or less and were omitted from this table.

[c] See footnote b, p. 83, and footnote a, p. 139.

sent a normal displacement of workers because of old age, death, retirement, or other natural causes. No data are available to show what would constitute such a normal displacement in the millinery trade. The table, however, would seem to indicate an abnormally unstable condition in millinery, since of all the workers employed in this representative group of shops for longer than one week in the year, 42 per cent appeared on the payroll less than ten weeks.

Each record of an individual in the calendar year is in reality the record of a job within that year, and the total earnings in the twelve months represent the total receipts of one job. Table 44 shows the receipts for 3,203 jobs, classified according to the type of work.

In Table 45 the total earnings are correlated with the duration of employment in one shop. Of course, the data in this table merely corroborate the facts already presented regarding irregularity of employment.

Even the group employed longest within the year received a median wage of only $388. For the group as a whole, the retail workers apparently earned much more than those in wholesale from a single job in the year—$165 as compared with $84. A larger proportion of the retail workers are employed twenty weeks or longer, and their rates of wages are higher.

It was in home interviews that we were able to find out more about the entire trade careers of

TABLE 44.—TOTAL EARNINGS DURING PERIOD OF EMPLOYMENT, BY OCCUPATIONS, FOR WOMEN EMPLOYED IN ANY ONE MILLINERY ESTABLISHMENT FOR MORE THAN ONE WEEK IN THE CALENDAR YEAR 1913

Total earnings	Women employed as												All women
	Forewomen	Designers	Trimmers	Copyists	Makers	Preparers	Improvers	Apprentices	Machine operators	Straw and crown sewers	Floor workers	Employes in all other manufacturing occupations	
Less than $25	..	1	23	273	79	118	25	139	15	7	20	8	708
$25 and less than $50	..	10	20	156	70	86	24	41	21	4	13	9	454
$50 and less than $75	..	2	12	75	38	41	18	22	10	4	10	11	243
$75 and less than $100	..	5	6	65	34	39	11	19	10	3	7	2	201
$100 and less than $150	2	7	12	82	45	39	21	15	11	4	9	9	256
$150 and less than $200	1	4	10	85	37	24	15	8	8	4	2	6	204
$200 and less than $250	1	4	6	70	20	24	11	2	5	4	7	1	155
$250 and less than $300	..	2	3	56	24	27	7	..	6	7	7	4	143
$300 and less than $350	2	4	2	58	30	6	5	..	7	7	8	3	132
$350 and less than $400	..	1	3	54	19	8	..	1	2	4	5	6	103
$400 and less than $450	1	3	2	56	18	8	..	..	5	3	4	5	105
$450 and less than $500	1	1	6	50	31	3	..	..	5	1	9	5	112
$500 and less than $600	6	4	12	63	52	..	..	..	16	3	9	1	166
$600 and less than $800	5	9	9	20	44	1	..	..	9	3	6	6	112
$800 and less than $1,000	7	2	2	6	9	..	..	..	..	..	1	6	33
$1,000 and less than $1,200	4	3	1	3	1	..	..	..	1	2	1	1	17
$1,200 and less than $1,500	3	7	4	1	..	..	..	..	1	..	..	1	17
$1,500 and less than $1,800	3	12	2	1	..	..	..	..	..	..	..	..	18
$1,800 or more	4	18	1	..	..	..	..	..	..	..	..	1	24
Total	40	99	136	1,174	551	424	137	247	132	60	118	85	3,203[a]
Median total earnings[b]	$829	$633	$129	$105	$163	$55	$78	$22	$145	$250	$150	$238	$99

[a] See footnote a, Table 42, p. 220.

[b] See footnote b, p. 83.

TABLE 45.—TOTAL EARNINGS DURING PERIOD OF EMPLOYMENT, BY MAIN BRANCHES OF THE TRADE AND BY NUMBER OF WEEKS ON THE PAYROLL, FOR WOMEN EMPLOYED IN ANY ONE MILLINERY ESTABLISHMENT FOR MORE THAN ONE WEEK IN THE CALENDAR YEAR 1913

Total earnings	Women employed in one establishment in the calendar year 1913									All women		
	More than 1 week but less than 10			10 weeks and less than 20			20 weeks or more					
	Retail	Wholesale	All branches	Retail	Wholesale	All branches	Retail	Wholesale	All branches	Retail	Wholesale	All branches
Less than $25	153	543	696	11	1	12	..	..	..	164	544	708
$25 and less than $50	70	334	404	30	18	48	2	..	2	102	352	454
$50 and less than $100	51	167	218	51	144	195	22	9	31	124	320	444
$100 and less than $200	10	26	36	75	192	267	61	96	157	146	314	460
$200 and less than $300	3	2	5	23	36	59	72	162	234	98	200	298
$300 and less than $400	..	..	..	8	8	16	65	154	219	73	162	235
$400 and less than $500	..	1	1	3	2	5	61	150	211	64	153	217
$500 and less than $600	1	..	1	1	1	2	67	96	163	69	97	166
$600 and less than $800	..	..	..	1	2	3	59	50	109	60	52	112
$800 and less than $1,000	..	..	..	..	..	..	19	14	33	19	14	33
$1,000 and less than $1,200	..	..	..	..	..	..	9	8	17	9	8	17
$1,200 and less than $1,500	..	..	..	..	..	..	11	6	17	11	6	17
$1,500 and less than $1,800	..	..	..	..	..	..	10	8	18	10	8	18
$1,800 or more	..	..	..	..	..	..	21	3	24	21	3	24
Total	288	1,073	1,361	203	404	607	479	756	1,235	970	2,233	3,203[a]
Median total earnings[b]	$25.53	$24.70	$24.44	$112.67	$120.31	$118.16	$428.69	$372.08	$388.36	$165.07	$84.45	$99.49

[a] See footnote a, Table 42, page 220.

[b] See footnote b, p. 83.

these girls, and especially whether or not they had been able to find other work in slack season. Table 46 shows for the girls whom we interviewed the length of their experience and their weekly wages in millinery.

Experience in the millinery trade, measured by the median, was four years and a half for the 242 women interviewed by us at home, and nearly six years for the 1,351 milliners reporting in the shops. The median earnings of the smaller group were almost identical, \$9.56, as compared with \$9.69 for all those recorded on current payrolls in the shops (Table 34, page 207), or \$10.02 for the group reporting length of experience in the trade (Table 41, page 218). The girls investigated in the shops were slightly older (as already discussed on page 121), with a median age of about twenty-two and a half as compared with nearly twenty-one for the smaller group. As to the duration of employment with the present firm, or the place of last employment, the median for our group was one year and ten months as compared with slightly more than two years for the larger number on the current payroll. In length of experience in the trade then, in time employed in the present establishment, and in age, the girls investigated in the shops had some advantage over those with whom we talked in their homes, although the latter were thoroughly typical in earning capacity. Moreover, those whom we interviewed were representative of the varied occupations of the industry. They

TABLE 46.—USUAL WEEKLY EARNINGS IN PRESENT OR LAST POSITION, BY YEARS IN THE TRADE, FOR MILLINERY WORKERS INTERVIEWED AT HOME

Weekly earnings	Women who have been in millinery									All women
	Less than 1 year	1 year and less than 2	2 years and less than 3	3 years and less than 5	5 years and less than 7	7 years and less than 10	10 years and less than 15	15 years and less than 20	20 years or more	
Less than $3	6	1	1	..	..	..	..	..	..	8
$3 and less than $4	1	4	..	..	..	..	..	..	..	5
$4 and less than $5	4	6	1	2	1	..	..	..	..	14
$5 and less than $6	2	5	4	4	..	..	..	..	..	15
$6 and less than $7	2	4	8	10	1	1	1	..	..	27
$7 and less than $8	..	3	3	7	3	1	..	..	..	17
$8 and less than $9	..	5	2	8	5	3	..	..	..	23
$9 and less than $10	..	..	1	13	5	1	1	..	1	22
$10 and less than $12	..	2	5	13	12	9	2	1	1	45
$12 and less than $15	..	..	2	4	13	18	12	1	2	52
$15 and less than $25	1	..	1	..	1	2	2	..	1	8
$25 or more	..	..	..	..	..	2	2	..	2	6
Total	16	30	28	61	41	37	20	2	7	242[a]
Median weekly earnings[b]	$4.25	$5.80	$7.00	$8.94	$10.92	$12.58	$13.50	$12.00	$14.25	$9.56

[a] Of the 252 women interviewed at home, five did not give information as to weekly wages in present or last position and five did not state number of years in the trade.

[b] See footnote b, p. 83.

included one forewoman, six designers and assistants, 26 trimmers, 80 copyists, 49 makers, 45 preparers, 13 improvers, 16 learners, and 16 in the other types of positions, such as machine operating, shopping, and the work of floor girls and errand girls. Their representative character from the point of view of positions and wages indicates that the data obtained from them with reference to annual income may safely be regarded as typical.

TABLE 47.—INCOMES IN PAST YEAR, BY NUMBER OF WEEKS EMPLOYED DURING YEAR, FOR MILLINERY WORKERS INTERVIEWED AT HOME

Income	Women employed				All women
	20 weeks and less than 30	30 weeks and less than 40	40 weeks and less than 50	50 weeks or more	
Less than $100	1	6	..	..	7
$100 and less than $200	4	3	7	1	15
$200 and less than $300	3	10	17	5	35
$300 and less than $400	..	16	16	8	40
$400 and less than $500	..	8	19	7	34
$500 and less than $600	..	1	14	10	25
$600 and less than $800	..	..	2	3	5
$800 and less than $1,000	..	..	2	..	2
$1,000 and less than $1,500	..	..	..	1	1
$1,500 and less than $2,000	..	..	2	..	2
$2,000 or more	..	..	..	2	2
Total	8	44	79	37	168[a]
Median income[b]	$125	$319	$397	$465	$368

[a] Of the 252 women interviewed at home, 18 had not been wage-earners for the full year, nine did not give information as to weeks worked in past year, 21 did not state year's income, and 36 failed to give information on either point.

[b] See footnote b, p. 83.

TABLE 48.—AVERAGE WEEKLY EARNINGS DURING PERIOD OF EMPLOYMENT OF WOMEN EMPLOYED IN ANY ONE MILLINERY ESTABLISHMENT FOR MORE THAN ONE WEEK IN THE CALENDAR YEAR 1913, FOR INDIVIDUAL WHOLESALE, RETAIL-WHOLESALE, AND RETAIL ESTABLISHMENTS

Number and type of establishment	Women earning												Median earnings[b]
	Less than $2	$2 and less than $4	$4 and less than $6	$6 and less than $8	$8 and less than $10	$10 and less than $12	$12 and less than $16	$16 and less than $20	$20 and less than $30	$30 and less than $40	$40 or more	Total	
Wholesale:													
I[a]	..	4	12	12	5	2	1	..	..	..	..	36	$6.25
II	4	2	9	10	6	7	8	2	2	1	..	51	8.17
III	1	5	13	17	8	14	10	1	1	1	..	71	7.92
IV	..	5	11	8	4	3	4	..	..	..	..	35	6.25
V	..	3	7	14	15	13	13	2	1	2	..	70	9.50
VI	..	5	5	10	12	11	18	15	12	2	1	91	12.50
VII	..	..	7	18	11	6	4	1	..	..	..	47	7.75
VIII	1	13	24	29	26	38	14	2	2	1	..	150	8.53
IX	1	8	36	32	29	34	10	..	..	1	..	151	7.63
X	..	4	3	8	27	24	14	2	1	1	2	86	10.06
XI	..	8	11	24	21	14	10	4	1	..	..	93	8.39
XII	..	1	1	3	11	16	15	3	4	..	..	54	11.17
XIII	4	45	83	87	46	25	27	4	3	..	1	325	6.60
XIV	7	23	48	38	25	19	13	4	1	1	1	180	6.50
XV	..	1	5	7	17	14	9	2	2	1	..	58	9.88
XVI	3	9	12	17	22	21	8	..	1	1	1	95	8.81
XVII	..	6	11	13	30	14	6	..	2	1	2	85	9.03
XVIII	8	25	33	26	29	17	12	5	3	1	..	159	6.83
XIX	..	5	40	53	46	26	17	5	3	1	..	196	8.00
XX	2	11	24	44	37	17	5	2	..	1	..	143	7.53
XXI	..	9	17	6	8	11	4	1	1	..	..	57	7.06
Total	31	192	412	476	435	346	222	55	40	16	8	2,233	8.03

Retail-wholesale:													
I	2	18	14	11	17	37	37	7	5	3	6	157	11.24
II	12	5	4	9	6	3	3	1	4	1	..	48	6.50
III	..	2	8	9	21	14	7	2	3	2	..	68	9.40
IV	3	18	11	9	8	13	34	4	6	2	5	113	11.08
V	6	8	4	6	6	5	21	13	5	1	8	83	13.58
VI	1	5	4	5	10	7	5	1	3	..	..	41	9.25
VII	..	1	8	16	8	..	2	..	..	1	..	36	6.75
Total	24	57	53	65	76	79	109	28	26	10	19	546	$9.95
Retail:													
I	3	2	6	1	2	2	5	..	1	3	..	25	8.50
II	8	5	3	4	1	2	1	..	2	..	..	26	5.00
III	3	8	3	6	4	4	3	..	1	..	..	32	6.50
IV	1	17	18	14	12	15	1	3	..	1	..	82	6.60
V	7	4	6	4	15	8	18	3	1	4	2	72	10.00
VI	..	3	2	2	4	2	..	..	2	..	..	15	8.17
VII	..	2	4	6	..	3	6	6	..	1	..	28	11.67
VIII	..	1	..	2	1	1	2	..	..	1	..	8	11.00
IX	4	15	9	13	1	2	4	1	3	..	..	52	5.50
X	..	11	2	6	3	8	2	..	..	..	1	33	6.44
XI	..	4	10	3	8	9	3	2	..	2	2	43	9.30
XII	..	..	..	1	2	1	3	..	1	..	..	8	12.00
Total	26	72	63	62	53	57	48	15	11	12	5	424	$7.50

[a] The Roman numerals represent individual establishments.

[b] See footnote b, p. 83, and footnote a, p. 139.

Table 47 shows annual income and the number of weeks of employment which these milliners were able to secure in all their positions in a year.

Thus the median income for those employed twenty to thirty weeks was $125; thirty to forty weeks, $319; forty to fifty, $397, while even for those at work fifty weeks or more, practically full time, the median was only $465.

Differences between shops are so great and so significant of the lack of standardization in the wage scale that it is worth while to show the wages paid in each shop. Table 48 gives these data.

That differences in the wage scale are not due to differences in hours of work is indicated in Table 49, showing median average weekly earnings by hours of labor.

In the 16 firms with a regular schedule of fifty-one hours and less than fifty-two a week, the median weekly earnings varied from less than $6.00 to $12 and over. Moreover, firms with the same general wage level, as for example the six in which the median earnings were between $9.00 and $10, varied in weekly hours from less than forty-eight to fifty-four.

One other factor in wages remains for discussion, namely, the age at beginning work. Advocates of child labor legislation say that the postponement of the time of beginning work increases the later earning capacity of the worker. Statistical data on this point are rare. To throw light on the question, we have divided the milliners into two groups:

TABLE 49.—MEDIAN AVERAGE WEEKLY EARNINGS IN 40 MILLINERY ESTABLISHMENTS, BY WEEKLY HOURS OF LABOR

Median average weekly earnings[a]	Establishments in which weekly hours of work were								All establishments
	Less than 48 hours	48 hours and less than 49	49 hours and less than 50	50 hours and less than 51	51 hours and less than 52	52 hours and less than 53	53 hours and less than 54	54 hours	
Less than $6	..	..	..	..	2	..	..	..	2
$6 and less than $7	..	..	..	..	5	..	2	3	10
$7 and less than $8	..	..	1	1	1	..	1	1	5
$8 and less than $9	..	..	..	..	3	1	1	2	7
$9 and less than $10	1	..	..	1	..	1	..	3	6
$10 and less than $11	..	..	..	..	..	..	1	1	2
$11 and less than $12	..	..	1	..	4	..	..	..	5
$12 or more	1	..	..	..	1	..	..	1	3
Total	2	..	2	2	16	2	5	11	40

[a] The average weekly earnings are based on the annual payroll, and were secured for each worker. The median of these average earnings has then been determined for each firm, and the firms are classified according to this median correlated with their weekly schedules of hours.

TABLE 50A.—WEEKLY WAGE RATES PAID TO MILLINERY WEEK WORKERS ON CURRENT PAYROLL, 1914, WHO BEGAN WORK UNDER 16 YEARS OF AGE, BY YEARS SINCE BEGINNING WORK

Weekly rate of wages	Women who had been wage-earners								All women
	Less than 1 year	1 year and less than 2	2 years and less than 3	3 years and less than 5	5 years and less than 10	10 years and less than 15	15 years and less than 20	20 years or more	
Less than $5	12	10	8	1	..	..	..	..	31
$5 and less than $6	..	7	6	5	1	1	..	..	20
$6 and less than $7	..	5	13	10	1	..	..	..	29
$7 and less than $8	1	1	7	25	10	..	..	1	45
$8 and less than $9	..	..	6	35	9	1	..	..	51
$9 and less than $10	..	..	2	14	21	2	..	..	39
$10 and less than $12	..	..	2	18	38	11	3	..	72
$12 and less than $15	..	..	..	4	67	37	5	5	118
$15 and less than $25	..	..	..	..	20	26	4	6	56
$25 or more	..	..	..	..	3	8	6	6	23
Total	13	23	44	112	170	86	18	18	484[a]
Median wage rate[b]	$2.71	$5.21	$6.62	$8.43	$12.22	$14.27	$17.50	$20.00	$10.75

[a] Of the 1,363 women who supplied personal records, 545 began work at sixteen years of age or over, 331 were piece workers, and three others did not state age at beginning work.

[b] See footnote b, p. 83, and footnote a, p. 139.

TABLE 50B.—WEEKLY WAGE RATES PAID TO MILLINERY WEEK WORKERS ON CURRENT PAY-ROLL, 1914, WHO BEGAN WORK AT 16 YEARS OF AGE OR OVER, BY YEARS SINCE BEGINNING WORK

Weekly rate of wages	Women who had been wage-earners								All women
	Less than 1 year	1 year and less than 2	2 years and less than 3	3 years and less than 5	5 years and less than 10	10 years and less than 15	15 years and less than 20	20 years or more	
Less than $5	24	17	5	4	..	..	..	..	50
$5 and less than $6	3	6	10	3	1	..	..	..	23
$6 and less than $7	..	8	8	10	1	..	..	..	27
$7 and less than $8	3	4	9	13	5	..	..	1	35
$8 and less than $9	1	6	7	17	14	5	..	..	50
$9 and less than $10	..	..	3	18	11	2	..	2	36
$10 and less than $12	1	..	2	23	27	4	4	1	62
$12 and less than $15	..	..	1	8	91	29	5	5	139
$15 and less than $25	..	..	..	3	26	34	10	7	80
$25 or more	..	..	..	..	11	18	12	2	43
Total	32	41	45	99	187	92	31	18	545[a]
Median wage rate[b]	$3.33	$5.75	$6.94	$9.14	$13.14	$16.76	$21.50	$15.00	$11.66

[a] Of the 1,363 women who supplied personal records, 484 began work under sixteen years of age, 331 were piece workers, and three others did not state age at beginning work.

[b] See footnote b, p. 83, and footnote a, p. 139.

those who began work before they were sixteen, and those who began at the age of sixteen or over. We then classified these groups according to the length of their experience and compared their median wages. The results are shown in Tables 50 A and 50 B.

For those who had been wage-earners less than a year, and who had begun work before they were sixteen, the median wage was $2.71 as compared with $3.33 for those who had postponed wage-earning until later. Similar differences hold true for every group except the last, with experience of twenty years or more. With this one exception, which might be explained in part by the small numbers included in it, the facts seem to point to an economic advantage to be gained by later entrance into industry.

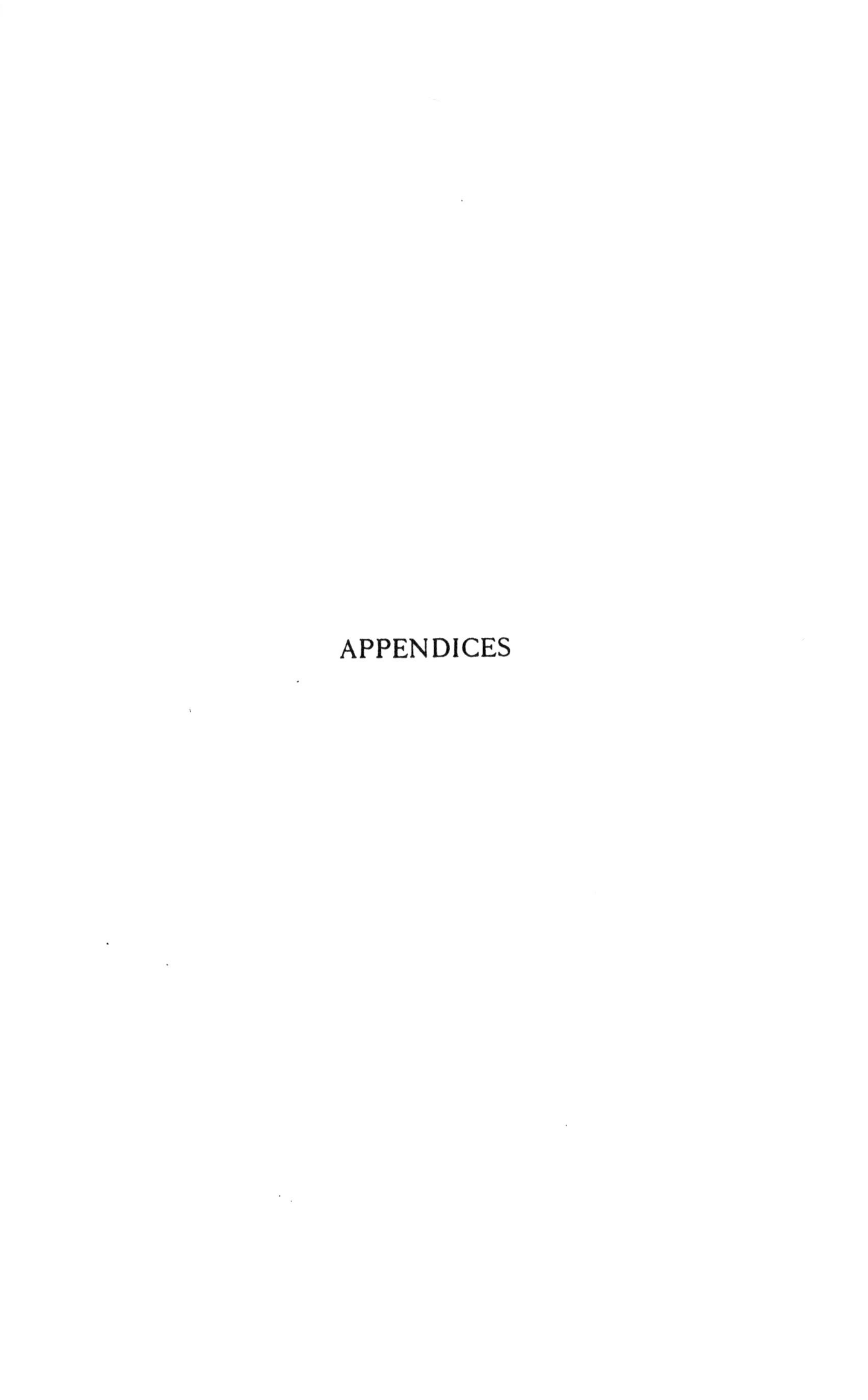

APPENDICES

APPENDIX A

RECORD CARDS USED IN THE INVESTIGATION

A. Number of Employes and Total Wages on Payroll each Week.

B (1). Individual Earnings on Payroll (Front of card).

B (2). Individual Earnings on Payroll (Back of card).

C. Record of Current Payroll Combined with Statements of Worker.

D. Questions Answered by Worker.

E. Record of Worker in Home Interview.

F. Work History (Home Interview).

G. Worker's Report of Shop (Home Interview).

H. Investigator's Report of Shop.

A. Number of Employes and Total Wages on Payroll Each Week

ESTABLISHMENT 24 | WAGES AND NUMBER OF EMPLOYEES. | N.Y.S.F.I.C.—FORM 6

PAYROLL PERIODS 6 DAYS EACH, COMMENCING January 8 1913 AGENT Walter

AVERAGE NUMBER OF EMPLOYEES 41 | AVERAGE WAGE PAYMENTS PER WEEK $586 | TOTAL WAGES $30,471 | AV. INDIVIDUAL WAGES PER WK. $

PAY-ROLL	NUMBER OF EMPLOYEES	TOTAL WAGES $	AVERAGE WAGES $	¢	PAY-ROLL	NUMBER OF EMPLOYEES	TOTAL WAGES $	AVERAGE WAGES $	¢
1	19	226			27	24	279		
2	15	219			28	25	269		
3	26	274			29	20	227		
4	23	338			30	15	175		
5	27	395			31	20	263		
6	29	438			32	34	447		
7	36	497			33	47	635		
8	39	568			34	49	679		
9	41	566			35	52	728		
10	47	639			36	52	756		
11	48	664			37	51	741		
12	49	679			38	50	732		
13	52	729			39	51	742		
14	55	798			40	51	742		
15	57	818			41	49	709		
16	56	816			42	51	730		
17	55	802			43	51	752		
18	53	771			44	48	721		
19	52	782			45	50	732		
20	49	701			46	50	738		
21	45	660			47	49	723		
22	39	646			48	43	697		
23	38	557			49	43	681		
24	37	473			50	43	639		
25	28	406			51	37	585		
26	27	377			52	35	510		

FORM 6—

B (1). Individual Earnings on Payroll (Front of Card)

ESTABLISHMENT 24 | EMPLOYEE'S NO. | INDIVIDUAL ANNUAL EARNINGS | AGENT WALTER | N.Y.S.F.I.C.–FORM 5.

NAME K———, E——— | ADDRESS ——— E. ——— St. | M16+ | M16− | F16+ X | F16−

OCCUPATION Maker

PAYROLL PERIODS 6 DAYS EACH, COMMENCING JAN 8 1913 191— | WEEKS WORKED 34 | EARNINGS $318 | AV. PER WEEK WORKED $ 9.35 | COMPUTED EARNINGS 52 WEEKS $ | COMPUTED 1/52 OF TOTAL ACTUAL EARNINGS $

PAY-ROLL	DAYS WORKED	HOURS WORKED	RATE OF PAY P	RATE OF PAY OTHER	NET EARNINGS $	NET EARNINGS ¢	ADDITIONS	DEDUCTIONS	PAY-ROLL	DAYS WORKED	HOURS WORKED	RATE OF PAY P	RATE OF PAY OTHER	NET EARNINGS $	NET EARNINGS ¢	ADDITIONS	DEDUCTIONS
1									14	6	54			10	—		
2	3	27		10 –	5	–			15	6	52½			9	72		
3	6	54			10	–			16	6	53			9	81		
4	6	54			10	–			17	6	54			10	–		
5	6	54			10	–			18	6	53			9	81		
6	6	54			10	–			19	6	54			10	–		
7	6	52			9	63			20	3	23¼			4	31	Laid off	
8	6	53			9	81			21								
9	6	54			10	–			22								
10	6	54			10	–			23								
11	6	49½			9	17			24								
12	6	53½			9	91			25								
13	6	54			10	—			26								

B (2). Individual Earnings on Payroll (Back of Card)

Establishment 24 | Employee's No. 70 | Name K——, E——

Pay-Roll	Days Worked	Hours Worked	Rate of Pay P	Rate of Pay Other	Net Earnings $	Net Earnings ¢	Additions	Deductions	Pay-Roll	Days Worked	Hours Worked	Rate of Pay P	Rate of Pay Other	Net Earnings $	Net Earnings ¢	Additions	Deductions
27									40	6	48½			8	98		
28									41	6	53			9	81		
29									42	6	54			10	–		
30									43	6	52			9	63		
31									44	6	53			9	81		
32									45	6	48½			8	98		
33	3	27		10 –	5	–			46	6	52			9	63		
34	6	54			10	–			47	6	53			9	81	Laid off	
35	6	54			10	–			48								
36	6	53			9	81			49								
37	6	53½			9	91			50								
38	6	54			10	–			51								
39	6	52			9	63			52								

C. Record of Current Payroll Combined With Statements of Worker

ESTABLISHMENT	EMPLOYEE'S NO	DEPARTMENT	N. Y. S. F. I. C. FORM 2
24	70	Milliniery	

NAME	K——, E——
ADDRESS	—E. —St. BOROUGH Manhattan
OCCUPATION	Maker

MALE	FEMALE	AGE
	X	19

CONJUGAL CONDITION				
S	M	W	D	N R
X				

RATE OF PAY	PIECE	HOUR	DAY	WEEK	½ MONTH	MONTH	ADDITIONS
		$0.	$	$ 10—	$	$	$

DAYS WORKED	REGULAR WEEKLY HOURS	HOURS WORKED THIS PERIOD	OVERTIME HOURS	UNDERTIME HOURS	EARNINGS THIS PERIOD	EARNINGS COMPUTED FOR REGULAR TIME	DEDUCTIONS
6	54	51	—	3	$ 9.44	$ 10.—	$

COUNTRY OF BIRTH	BEGAN WORK	TIME AT WORK	IN THIS TRADE	THIS FIRM
U. S.	AGE 14	5 yrs.	5 yrs.	1 yr.

AT HOME	BOARD	PAYROLL PERIOD
X		6 DAYS ENDING Jan. 21, 1914.

D. Questions Answered by Worker

NEW YORK STATE FACTORY COMMISSION.

FORM 1

ESTABLISHMENT 24 | EMPLOYEE'S NO. 70 | DEPARTMENT Millinery

K———, E——— | MALE OR FEMALE? F

ADDRESS 430 East X St. BOROUGH Mann. | ARE YOU SINGLE, MARRIED WIDOWED OR DIVORCED? single

COUNTRY OF BIRTH California AGE 19 YEARS

HOW OLD WERE YOU WHEN YOU BEGAN TO WORK FOR WAGES? 14 YEARS

HOW LONG HAVE YOU BEEN IN THIS TRADE OR BUSINESS? 5 yrs.

HOW LONG HAVE YOU BEEN WORKING FOR THIS FIRM? 1 yr.

WHAT IS YOUR REGULAR WORK HERE? Milliner

DO YOU LIVE AT HOME? Yes. DO YOU BOARD?

E. Record of Worker in Home Interview

SURNAME K- - - FIRST NAME E- - - ADDRESS --E. --- St. FLOOR 2d. EMPLOYMENT Millinery

AGE 19 DATE OF BIRTH (NUMERALS) 2 -- '95 (MO. DAY YR.) CONJUGAL CONDITION Single NATIVITY U.S. Cal. City (DISTRICT CITY OR COUNTRY?) YEARS IN U.S. Life IN NEW YORK 8

REASON FOR COMING TO NEW YORK Father moved here OCCUPATION BEFORE COMING None

NATIVITY OF FATHER U.S. DISTRICT California NATIVITY OF MOTHER Germany DISTRICT Not stated

SCHOOL HISTORY	SPECIAL TRAINING			
	NAME OF SCHOOL	DATES ENTERED	DATES LEFT	SUBJECTS
SCHOOLS ATTENDED -- San Francisco (STATE PLACE) FOREIGN U.S. NOT N.Y.C. N.Y.C. # (CHECK)				
LAST SCHOOL N.Y. (PLACE) P.S. #-- (NAME OR NUMBER) 6 B (GRADE) '09 (DATE OF LEAVING) 14 (AGE) PRIVATE, PAROCHIAL, PUBLIC	PUBLIC EVENING None			
YEARS IN SCHOOL 7 Didn't like N.Y. schools (REASON FOR LEAVING)	BUSINESS "			
AGE AT BEGINNING WORK 14 DATE OF WORKING PAPERS At leaving school	TRADE "			
WORK BEFORE LEAVING SCHOOL None YRS. AT WORK 5 YRS. IN TRADE IND. 5	OTHER "			

HOME WITH FAMILY: (CHECK) FATHER # MOTHER # SISTERS # BROTHERS HUSBAND CHILDREN WITH OTHER RELATIVES --- RELATIONSHIP TO HEAD OF FAMILY BOARDING --- PLACE COST PER WEEK

MEMBERSHIP TRADE UNION None DUES --- CHURCH CLUB None USE OF FREE TIME Sews a little VACATION WITH PAY None

WEEKS OUT OF WORK IN PAST YEAR 16 (1913) DUE TO SLACK SEASON 16 PART TIME 0 VACATION: HOLIDAYS (WITHOUT PAY) 0 0 QUITTING JOB 0 ILLNESS OF SELF 0 OTHER CAUSES 0 TOTAL 16

BUDGET ESTIMATED YEARLY INCOME $328 EARNINGS IN PAST WEEK $10 WEEKLY EXPENSES (PAST WEEK) CONTRIBUTION TO HOME $4 INSURANCE None CARFARE 30 cts. LUNCHES Takes from home SPENDING MONEY ALLOWED Manages her own earnings

PHYSICAL CONDITION Apparently good DEFECTS NOTED None COMPLAINT None

REFERRED TO FOR MEDICAL TREATMENT None FOR WORK None FOR OTHER AID None

NAME GIVEN BY Payroll record LANGUAGE SPOKEN BY WORKER English MOTHER English OTHER RECORD FORM NO. 5, 12, & payroll data

DATE 3/26/14 INVESTIGATOR E. L. Meigs SOURCE OF INFORMATION Girl at home

COMMITTEE ON WOMEN'S WORK. FORM 4, DEC. '11.—WORKER

F. Work History (Home Interview)

SURNAME	FIRST NAME	ADDRESS	FLOOR	EMPLOYMENT
K- - -	E- - -	-- E. --- St.	2d	Millinery

DATE EMPLOYED	TIME HELD	NAME AND ADDRESS OF FIRM	BUSINESS	KIND OF WORK	WEEKLY EARNINGS TIME	WEEKLY EARNINGS PIECE	HOW FOUND	REASON FOR LEAVING	TIME IDLE AFTER LEAVING
FROM - '09 TO - '09	2 wks	NAME S----- ADDRESS Broadway & 100th St.	Dressmaking	Putting stays in linings	$1.00 #$1.25		Ad.	Didn't like it	None
- '09 12/12	4 yrs	L----- -- E. 60th St.	Millinery- retail	Errands Improver	$2.50 #$7.00		Ad.	For better work	None
1/9/13 5/17/13	4 mo	T----- & Co. -- Fifth Ave.	Millinery- retail	Maker	#$10		Friend	Laid off; slack	2½mo
7/13 8/13	2 wks	H----- -- E. 50th St.	Candy mfg.	Packing and tying bows	#$5.00		Sister	Didn't like it	None
8/10/13 11/15/13	3 mo	T----- & Co. -- Fifth Ave.	Millinery retail	Maker	#$10		Sent for	Laid off; slack	6wk
1/7/14		" " "	"	"	#$10		"	" (Still employed)	

DATE	INVESTIGATOR	SOURCE OF INFORMATION
3/26/14	E. L. Meigs	Girl and mother at home

COMMITTEE ON WOMEN'S WORK. FORM 5. DEC. '11.—WORK HISTORY

G. Worker's Report of Shop (Home Interview)

NAME OF FIRM	ADDRESS	BUSINESS	FLOOR
T----- & Co.	-- Fifth Ave.	Gowns and hats DEPARTMENT Millinery	3rd

NAME OF WORKER K- - - E- - - ADDRESS -- E. --- St. 1/9/13 (DATE OF ENTERING; LEAVING) Employed · U.S. (NATIONALITY) · 2-'95 (DATE OF BIRTH)

PROCESSES OF WORK Making · POSTURE AT WORK Sits

TRAINING IN WORKROOM Came as experienced worker (BY WHOM GIVEN · KIND OF WORK · LENGTH OF TRAINING)

WEEKLY WAGES $10 T. # P. (FIRST IN THIS ESTABLISHMENT;) $10 T# P. (LAST) No overtime T. P. (MAXIMUM WITHOUT OVERTIME) T. P. (MAXIMUM WITH OVERTIME) $10 T. # P. (IF STILL HERE, WAGE LAST WEEK)

FINES ½ hr. for more than 15 min. (RATE FOR LATENESS) None (SPOILED WORK) None (OTHER) · CHARGES FOR SUPPLIES None · VACATION WITH PAY None (NO. WEEKS)

REGULARITY IN PAST 12 MOS. WEEKS LOST, IN THIS JOB, DUE TO: 18 (SLACK SEASON) 0 (PART TIME) 0 (VACATION; HOLIDAYS (WITHOUT PAY)) 0 (ILLNESS (SELF)) 0 (OTHER CAUSES) 0 · 2 wks (TIME IN OTHER JOBS) · 16 (TOTAL LOST)

HOURS OF LABOR 8 A. M. (NORMAL BEGIN) 6 P. M. (END) 6 P. M. (SATURDAY) 1 HR. (NOON) 9 HRS. (TOTAL DAILY) 54 HRS. (TOTAL WEEKLY) · REMARKS None (NOTE VARIATIONS FROM NORMAL SCHEDULE)

OVERTIME None (NUMBER OF TIMES PER WEEK) -- P. M. (CLOSING HR.) -- P. M. (SATURDAY) -- MIN. (SUPPER) -- HRS. (TOTAL DAILY) -- HRS. (TOTAL WEEKLY) ----- (SEASON OF OVERTIME IN YEAR) -- (RATE OF PAY)

HOME WORK None (KIND) -- (HOURS) -- (EARNINGS) --- (HOUSE LICENSED?)

WORK ROOM Gas stove provided (LUNCH ROOM PRIVILEGES) Good (DRESSING ROOM) Good (TOILETS (CONDITION)) Good (LIGHTING) Bottled (DRINKING WATER)

ILLEGAL EMPLOYMENT OF WORKER None

DATE 3/26/14 · INVESTIGATOR E. L. Meigs · SOURCE OF INFORMATION Girl at home

COMMITTEE ON WOMEN'S WORK. FORM 12, DEC. '11.—WORKER'S RECORD OF FACTORY

H. Investigator's Report of Shop

NAME: T—— & Co. ADDRESS: -- Fifth Ave. FLOORS: Whole building 5 floors

BUSINESS: Gowns and hats DEPARTMENT INVESTIGATED: Millinery FLOOR: 3rd

PROCESSES OF WORK FOR WOMEN	NUMBER	MAX. WAGE	T OR P.	POSTURE
Apprentices	5	$3	T	Sit
Improvers	3	6	T	"
Preparers	5	9	T	"
Makers	29	18	T	"
Designers and trimmers	6	67	T	"
Feather curlers	2	25	T	"
Stock clerks	7	14	T	"

BUILDING: Mercantile (TYPE) Five (NO. OF FLOORS) Wooden (STAIR CONSTRUCTION) Passenger (ELEVATOR)

NATURE OF PRODUCT: Retail hats

MARKET FOR GOODS: High grade 5 Ave. trade —S. AT THIS ADDRESS: 15½

WOMEN'S WAGES: Designing (BEST PAID PROCESS) $67 (MAX. WAGE) Apprentice (LOWEST PAID PROCESS) $2 (MIN WAGE)

WAGES OF LARGEST GROUP: $9

FINES: For lateness CHARGES FOR SUPPLIES: None

WOMEN EMPLOYED: 57 (MAX. FORCE) 14 (MIN. AGE) Regular (REGULARITY OF ATTENDANCE) Long (AV. YRS. OF EMPLOYMENT) 83 (NO. PASSING THROUGH IN A YEAR) NO. OF MEN: ——

NATIONALITIES (WOMEN): American & French (PREDOMINANT) —— (OTHER) ITALIANS: None —— (YRS. EMPLOYED) —— (EFFICIENCY) —— (COMPARATIVE WAGES) —— (ENGLISH REQUIRED)

LEARNERS: 12 (NO. PER YEAR) —— (NO. SUCCESSFUL) 14 (MIN AGE) NO. —— $2 (FIRST WAGE) T. #/ PROCESSES At least 2 seasons (LENGTH OF TRAINING) By head of table (PLAN OF TRAINING)

TRADE SCHOOL TRAINING: "No good" (DESIRABILITY) (FEASIBILITY) SCARCITY OF EXPERIENCED WORKERS: Yes TRADE UNION: None

BUSY SEASON: March-May 30; Aug.20-Dec.1 (MONTHS) 2 weeks (LENGTH OF EMPLOYMENT OF MAX. FORCE) 15 (MIN. FORCE IN PAST YEAR) POLICY REGARDING WOMEN: None MEN: None

HOURS: 8 A. M. (BEGIN) 6 P. M. (END) 6 P. M. (SATURDAY) 1 HR. (NOON) 9 HRS. (TOTAL DAILY) 54 HRS. (TOTAL WEEKLY) SUMMER 12 P. M. (SATURDAY) 44 HRS (TOTAL WEEKLY) WEEKS PART TIME —— WEEKS WITHOUT WORKERS Yes

OVERTIME: 1 or 2 (EVENINGS PER WEEK) 7 P. M. (CLOSING HR.) —— MIN. (SUPPER) 10 HRS. (TOTAL DAILY) 55-56 HRS. (TOTAL WEEKLY) No (ENTIRE FORCE KEPT?) Time (RATE OF PAY) PAYMENT FOR SAT. HALF HOLIDAYS: Yes No (PAYMENT FOR HOLIDAYS AND VACATION)

HOMEWORK: None (SEASON) —— (PROCESSES) —— (NO. OF FAMILIES) —— (LOCATION) —— (SHOP EMPLOYES) —— (EMPLOYER'S OPINION OF THE SYSTEM) ——

WORKROOM: Good (LIGHTING) Sun (KIND) Windows (VENTILATING SYSTEM) Adequate (SPACE) (CLEANLINESS) —— (CLEANING SYSTEM) None (NOISE) Yes (SEATS WITH BACKS) None (OCCUPATIONAL DANGERS)

DATE: 1/26 & 28/14 INVESTIGATOR: H. R. Walter SOURCE OF INFORMATION: Bookkeeper, treasurer of company and payrolls

COMMITTEE ON WOMEN'S WORK. FORM 13. DEC. '12. RECORD OF WORKPLACE.

APPENDIX B

NOTE ON WAGES OF STRAW-BRAID SEWERS

IN 1907 the New York State Department of Labor published in its bulletin* the payroll of a representative straw-hat manufacturer in New York City, and summarized in a general way the seasons and wages in this industry. The payroll quoted covered the second and third weeks of January of that year. It showed in the first week that of the 19 straw sewers employed, 6 women earned less than $20, 9 earned from $20 to $30, and 4 earned $30 or more. In the second week 5 women received less than $20, 10 between $20 and $30, and again 4 received $30 or more. The lowest earnings recorded were $10.50, which are so far below those of the rest of the workers that it might well be assumed that this worker was a beginner. The highest wage paid in either week was $36.90, and the median earnings for the first week were $23.89 and for the second $24.50.

The labor inspector who reported on this trade estimated that only 15 per cent of the 2,000 women employed during the busy season find work at straw sewing during the entire year, but that their earnings vary, approximating $35 per week in the first four months of the year, $18 per week in the succeeding four months, and $12 per week in the last third of the year. Sixty per cent work at straw sewing four months at about $20 a week and four months at trimming felt hats at about $12 a week. They must find employment outside the hat trade for the other four months. The remaining 25

* New York State Department of Labor, New York Labor Bulletin, March, 1907. Whole No. 32, pp. 57–58.

per cent he believed to be married women who give all or the greater part of their time to straw sewing during the height of the season, which averages four months in length, earning about $22 a week for this period, and then return to their homes for the rest of the year.

Attention was also called in the bulletin to advertisements in the New York *World* for straw sewers capable of earning $30 to $35 a week. The employers preferred workers capable of earning this amount, since they give a larger output for the space and machine power used. Straw sewers of course are practically all piece workers. Hence the size of their earnings depends largely on their speed and skill in operating the machines. Although this report is not of very recent date, it serves nevertheless to indicate the general tendency of conditions in this occupation. All evidences point to the possibility and even to the prevalence of unusually high earnings for women in this trade, though the maximum wages are possible only for the short four months' season.

H. R. Walter.

APPENDIX C

WAGES IN MILLINERY WORKROOMS OF DEPARTMENT STORES IN NEW YORK CITY AND IN EIGHT UP-STATE CITIES

IN THE investigation of wages in department stores made by the New York State Factory Investigating Commission in New York City and in eight other important cities in New York state,—namely, Buffalo, Rochester, Syracuse, Utica, Schenectady, Albany, Troy, and Kingston,—payroll statistics were secured for the millinery workrooms in these establishments.*

Twenty-one stores were covered in New York City and 34 in the eight other cities. In the former, records for 150 milliners were secured and in the latter for 245. These records do not represent the total force in the 55 workrooms, since the returns in many cases were incomplete.

The workroom force, however, in the millinery department of a dry goods store is usually small. The trimmed hats sold in this section are purchased as finished products from the wholesaler, and the actual creation of hats rarely takes place here. The work consists in the trimming of "shapes" bought in the store, the occasional alteration of a trimmed hat to suit the customer's taste, and the even more occasional making up of a special order or of a stock hat. Some original work is done in these workrooms, however, since among the

* These statistics were included in the department store tabulation and were also separately tabulated and published as an appendix to the report on wages in the millinery trade in the 1915 report of the Factory Investigating Commission. (New York State Factory Investigating Commission, Fourth Report, 1915. Vol. II, pp. 449–467.) The data were tabulated separately for New York City and for the up-state cities.

150 workers for whom records were secured in New York City there were 14 designers. The fact that six of the 14 received wages under $20 a week indicates, however, that the title "designer" was, at least in some instances, a misnomer. There is little work for a real designer, since both the "ready-to-wear" and the "pattern" hats are made in the wholesale shops or the large retail establishments which sell models to the trade.

All the occupations which were found in the retail millinery establishments were represented in the workrooms of the department stores,—forewomen, apprentices, designers, makers, improvers, floor girls, flower and feather hands, and so forth,—though the proportions in each occupation varied in the two branches. It is the retail millinery shops, in fact, which the department store workrooms most closely resemble in processes of work and in the product of the workroom.

In the matter of wages we find the median earnings for the New York City stores about half way between earnings in the retail and the wholesale millinery shops in Manhattan. The median in the New York stores is $10.20, as compared with $10.90 in the retail and $9.41 in the wholesale branches of the trade.* The department store median is higher, however, than that of the retail millinery shops, which is $9.30, and lower than that of the large retail establishments with wholesale business, which is $12.09. These medians are based on actual earnings in a typical week, taken from the current payrolls of the shops investigated. The median earnings in the stores up-state are of course lower than those in New York City, namely, $8.71.

The wage rates prevailing in department store workrooms, as in the millinery establishments, are higher than the actual earnings, as is shown in the following median rates: $10.75 in department store workrooms in New York City, $8.76 in up-state workrooms, and $12.04 in retail, and $10.51 in wholesale millinery establishments in Manhattan. Since the

* See Supplementary Report, Table 34, p. 207.

returns for the department store workrooms were not complete, and may therefore have included a disproportionate number either of the higher or of the lower paid workers, and also since these groups are not large, the wage figures should be used with caution. However, in view of the differences brought out by the medians, it is fair to assume that they indicate the general trend of wages in these types of work. In comparing the proportion of workers earning less than $5.00 a week, we find 15.9 per cent earning under this amount in department stores in Buffalo, Rochester, and the six other cities, only 10 per cent in the New York City department stores, and 14.4 per cent in the millinery establishments of Manhattan. Again, among the higher paid workers, the New York City department store workrooms lead with 26 per cent earning $15 or more, the up-state workrooms and the millinery establishments in New York City being on a par with 15.1 and 15.2 per cent respectively in this group. In the highest wage group, $30 or more, we find only 2 per cent for department store workrooms both in New York City and up-state, as compared with 3.3 per cent in the millinery shops as a whole, and 7.7 per cent in the large retail establishments, the group in which the very high salaried positions are found. The wage level in the New York City workrooms then compares favorably with wages paid in all other branches of the millinery trade in the city. As might be expected, those in the smaller cities fell somewhat below this standard.

Statistics were also secured from the department store workers regarding age, nationality, years of experience in millinery, years at work, years with present establishment, and age at beginning work. A comparison of the ages of the women in these workrooms with those of the workers included in the millinery investigation proper shows a smaller proportion of girls under 25 in the former than in the latter,—56 per cent in New York City and 52 per cent in up-state workrooms as compared with 69 per cent in Manhattan millinery establishments. In tabulating the age at beginning work, it was found that none of the workers in the New York City store workrooms had started their work careers before reaching the age of fourteen. Only 30 per cent of the up-state milliners had begun work under sixteen, as compared with 40 per cent of the workers in millinery workrooms in New York City department stores and 45 per cent in wholesale and retail millinery shops. The proportion of foreign-born workers is also much larger in the millinery shops than in either the New York City or up-state department store workrooms, 41 per cent as compared with 14 per cent and 10 per cent respectively.

Data as to workroom conditions, hours of work, holidays, vacations, and the like were not covered in this tabulation, since they were included in the report on department stores of the Factory Investigating Commission.

H. R. WALTER.

APPENDIX D

THE WAGES BOARD FOR MILLINERS IN VICTORIA

Correspondence with the Chief Factory Inspector

July 31, 1915.

Chief Inspector of Factories,
Melbourne, Australia.
Dear Sir:

We have been making an investigation of wages in the millinery trade in New York City and we are much interested in the possibility of wage legislation in this trade.

We are desirous of securing exact information about the operation of the minimum wage law as it affects the millinery trade in Victoria. We are anxious to utilize such information in a forthcoming book. I should greatly appreciate any information you might give me, especially that covering the following points:

1. How extensive is the millinery trade in Victoria? We find that the official returns in the published reports include dressmakers and milliners, so that we cannot determine the number in the millinery shops alone.
2. What are the general characteristics of the trade in Victoria as to number of employes per shop, extent of the millinery industry, and the market for the goods, whether local or extensive?
3. Were the members of the wage board appointed by the government or elected as representatives of the workers and employers, and if the latter, how is the election accomplished, especially in the case of the employes?

4. What was the process of determining the award and what factors entered into the decision? We should like to know especially whether facts regarding irregularity of employment were taken into consideration in determining wage rates.
5. What are the facts about irregularity of employment, how long do the seasons last and what proportion of the workers is kept in dull season?
6. Is it possible to give any data showing the effect of the legislation on the millinery trade? Have the numbers decreased in the trade as a whole? Has the pay of the better paid workers been reduced? What proportion of the workers has received increases? How many violations of the law have been prosecuted within a stated period, possibly the last year for which the facts are available? What have been the results of the prosecutions?

I realize that we are asking for very comprehensive information, but it is of great importance to us to be able to have first-hand information regarding wage legislation in this trade in Victoria.

Under separate cover I am sending you a copy of a pamphlet which we prepared on wages in the millinery trade for the New York State Factory Investigating Commission.

Very sincerely yours,

(Sgd.) MARY VAN KLEECK.

Chief Inspector of Factories' Office,
Government Offices, Spring Street,
Melbourne, 17th September, 1915

Madam:

I have pleasure in supplying the following information in reply to the questions asked in your letter of the 31st July:

1. Particulars extending over a number of years will be found in Return No. 1 attached.

2. The number of employes per shop is shown in Return No. 2.

   The market for the goods is solely an Australasian one, therefore the output is limited. The State of Victoria manufactures more than any other State in the Commonwealth, but, notwithstanding the high duty on millinery goods, it is often impossible to produce them as cheaply as they can be landed in Australia with the duty paid. One reason is that, when the summer season in England is an unfavorable one, the unsold goods of manufacturers there are sent out to Australia at practically any price, and the protective duty is of little value, as they can be landed here in many cases for about the cost of the material. This means loss of work to the workers and the prevention of trade expansion.

3. When new members were appointed to the Millinery Board in 1913, nominations were asked for in the Public Press. More names were submitted than were required, and the Minister selected five employers and five employes, and nominated them for appointment.

   If one-fifth of the employers or employes had lodged an objection within twenty-one days to the persons nominated as their representatives, an election would have been held. No objection came to hand in this case, and the persons nominated were duly appointed.

   When an election is held, employers are required to supply lists of employes of eighteen years of age and upwards, and from these the roll is compiled. The election is conducted by this office, and the voting is by post.

4. The five representatives of employers and five representatives of employes met and nominated a Chairman who was subsequently appointed by the Governor-in-Council. The full Board then met with the Chairman, and the minimum wage was the first subject of

discussion. The determining factor in fixing the minimum was the lowest amount upon which a girl could live in this State if she had to keep herself.

The amount of lost time was also taken into consideration, and, as other trades akin to this had at that time fixed a minimum of 16s. per week of 48 hours, it was considered that, if a wage of 20s. was fixed, this would allow of some provision being made for lost time. As the cost of living increased in the State, the minimum wage was raised to 25s. per week of 48 hours.

5. In Victoria the millinery season usually extends for a period of about thirty-nine weeks in the year, but many of the employes within the Metropolitan area contrive to get employment for longer periods through the following causes:

The large wholesale warehouses in Melbourne import their models from London and the Continent, and then do all their millinery on the premises. As the wholesale season starts nearly two months before the retail season, a number of employes work first in the wholesale warehouses and then go on to the retail, and are thus enabled to get work nearly all the year round.

The proportion working in the warehouses during the slack season would not be more than 25 per cent, but in other factories, generally speaking, a higher proportion of employes would be kept, though no statistics are available to prove what the percentage is.

6. (a) Factories Legislation has not had the effect of decreasing the number of workers.

The Determination of the Board came into operation in the year 1907. Return No. 3 attached shows that in 1906 the number of workers before the coming into operation of the Determination, for whom returns were supplied, was 1,505. Return No. 1, commencing from 1907 (the first year that the Determination was in operation), shows an increase in this number, and a further increase is shown in the following years.

During the next three years a decrease is shown but this decrease is only in the juvenile labour employed, the number of persons earning the minimum wage and over having increased from 287 in 1907 to 364 in 1912. Included in the latter should also be 63 piece workers who were formerly included with minimum wage workers, and which would bring the number up to 427. This decrease of juvenile workers was partly owing to an amendment of the law, which raised the age at which a girl might be allowed to work in a factory from thirteen years to fifteen years. Permission to be employed at fourteen years might be obtained in necessitous cases. The numbers are again on the up grade, and show increases for the last two years.

(b) That the pay of the workers has been considerably increased is shown by Returns Nos. 1 and 3.

Return No. 3 shows the average earned by all workers in the trade, prior to the coming into operation of the Determination, to be 10s. 10d. for all women and girls employed, while No. 1 shows a steady increase each year since the Determination came into operation until in 1914 the average wage reached 17s. 11d.

The better paid workers also show a large increase. In 1906 the average wage for adults was 21s. 4d., while in 1914 the wage for these employes (including piece workers) was 31s. 2d.

(c) The attached Returns show that the whole of the workers have received increases.

(d) There has been no difficulty in securing compliance with the Determination of the Board for this trade, and very few breaches have come under notice.

A copy of the Determination is attached.

I have the honor to be,

Madam,

Your obedient Servant,

(Sgd.) H. M. MURPHY,

Chief Inspector of Factories.

RETURN NO. 1A.—WOMEN EMPLOYED IN THE MILLINERY TRADE IN VICTORIA, BY CLASS AND AGE OF WORKERS, FOR EACH YEAR SINCE THE APPOINTMENT OF A WAGE BOARD. 1907–1914

Class and age of workers	Women employed in								Per cent increase or decrease in women employed from 1907 to 1914
	1907	1908	1909	1910	1911	1912	1913	1914	
Apprentices and improvers									
14 years and less than 15	46	37	7	6	5	2	6	7	−84.8
15 years and less than 16	101	133	121	132	118	87	117	104	+ 3.0
16 years and less than 17	165	208	210	191	168	136	161	200	+21.2
17 years and less than 18	233	194	236	199	222	153	133	170	−27.0
18 years and less than 19	228	221	215	203	188	155	140	143	−37.3
19 years and less than 20	182	195	208	184	169	140	148	130	−28.6
20 years and less than 21	135	202	188	141	137	116	129	110	− 18.5
21 years or more	186	218	265	261	183	148	113	117	−37.1
Total	1,276	1,408	1,450	1,317	1,190	937	947	981	−23.1
"Minimum wage workers"[a]	287	319	360	379	396	364	456	496	+89.9
Piece workers[b]	..	..	..	..	69	63	32	49	
Grand total	1,563	1,727	1,810	1,696	1,655	1,364	1,435	1,526	− 2.4

[a] "Minimum wage workers" are the experienced workers who have passed the stage of apprentice and improver, and are eligible to the full minimum rate.

[b] Piece workers are included with "minimum wage workers" until 1911.

RETURN NO. IB.—AVERAGE WEEKLY WAGES OF WOMEN EMPLOYED IN THE MILLINERY TRADE IN VICTORIA, BY CLASS AND AGE OF WORKERS, FOR EACH YEAR SINCE THE APPOINTMENT OF A WAGE BOARD. 1907–1914

Class and age of workers	Average wages in								Per cent increase in average wages from 1907 to 1914
	1907	1908	1909	1910	1911	1912	1913	1914	
	s. d.	s. d.	s. d.	s. d.	s. d.	s. d.	s. d.	s. d.	
Apprentices and improvers									
14 years and less than 15	2 9	2 9	2 11	2 6	3 8	2 6	4 2	5 ..	81.8
15 years and less than 16	3 2	3 ..	2 9	3 5	2 10	3 1	4 3	5 5	71.1
16 years and less than 17	4 2	3 9	3 10	3 11	4 4	4 2	4 9	6 3	50.0
17 years and less than 18	5 7	5 5	4 10	5 11	5 8	6 4	6 10	8 ..	43.3
18 years and less than 19	7 5	7 2	6 10	7 10	7 7	7 8	9 1	10 3	38.2
19 years and less than 20	8 9	9 4	9 6	9 4	9 6	9 11	11 1	12 4	41.0
20 years and less than 21	10 1	11 6	12 ..	11 9	11 6	12 7	13 2	15 4	52.1
21 years or more	12 ..	12 4	12 6	14 10	13 9	14 ..	14 4	16 5	36.8
Total	7 4	7 8	7 10	8 6	7 11	8 5	8 11	10 1	37.5
"Minimum wage workers"[a]	31 4	29 10	30 3	31 5	31 3	32 4	32 1	33 2 [c]	2.1
Piece workers[b]	..	..	..	..	19 1	20 1	22 5	20 1 [c]	
Grand total	11 9	11 9	12 3	13 7	14 ..	15 4	16 7	17 11	52.5

[a] "Minimum wage workers" are the experienced workers who have passed the stage of apprentice and improver and are eligible to the full minimum rate.

[b] Piece workers are included with "minimum wage workers" until 1911.

[c] In 1914 the average wage of the group including both "minimum wage workers" and piece workers, was 32s.

RETURN NO. 2.—SIZE OF MILLINERY ESTABLISHMENTS IN VICTORIA. 1914

Number of employes	Establishments
From 1 to 5	83
From 6 to 10	27
From 11 to 15	22
From 16 to 20	9
From 21 to 30	6
From 31 to 40	5
From 41 to 50	4
From 51 to 100	..
Over 100	1
Total	157

RETURN NO. 3.—AVERAGE WEEKLY WAGES PAID AND NUMBER OF WOMEN EMPLOYED, BY AGES, IN THE MILLINERY TRADE IN VICTORIA. 1906[a]

Age	Women	Average wage	
		s.	d.
14 years and less than 15	23	3	..
15 years and less than 16	80	3	11
16 years and less than 17	195	4	..
17 years and less than 18	229	5	4
18 years and less than 19	225	6	8
19 years and less than 20	188	8	11
20 years and less than 21	113	10	2
21 years or more	452	21	4
Total	1,505	10	10

[a] The Determination of the Milliners' Board first came into operation in the following year.

[Extract from *Victoria Government Gazette*, No. 155, of 10th October, 1913, pages 4539 and 4540.]

FACTORIES AND SHOPS ACTS

DETERMINATION OF THE MILLINERS' BOARD

In accordance with the provisions of the Factories and Shops Acts, the Special Board appointed to determine the lowest prices or rates of payment to be paid for wholly or partly preparing or manufacturing, either inside or outside a factory or work-room, the following articles, that is to say:—

> "Women's, girls', and infants' bonnets, caps, and hats, other than straw hats not made on wire shapes or frames, and other than felt hats, but including the trimming of straw hats"

has made the following Determination, namely:—

1. That previous Determinations of this Board are hereby amended, and such amendments shall come into force and be operative on and after 3rd November, 1913.

The Determination and amendments are printed hereunder.

WAGES

2. That the following shall be the lowest rate of wages to be paid to—All adults, 25s. per week of 48 hours.

APPRENTICES AND IMPROVERS

"Apprentice" means any person under twenty-one years of age bound by indentures of apprenticeship, or any person over twenty-one years of age, who, with the sanction of the Minister, is bound by indentures of apprenticeship. (Act 2386, Section 5.)

"Improver" means any person (other than an apprentice) who does not receive a piece-work price or a wages rate fixed by any Special Board for persons other than apprentices or improvers, and who is not over twenty-one years of age, or who being over twenty-one years of age holds a licence from the Minister to be paid as an improver. (Act 2386, Section 5.)

3. That—

   (a) The lowest rates which may be paid to an apprentice or an improver; and

   (b) The proportionate number of apprentices and improvers who may be employed by any employer

shall be as shown in the following table:—

Wages per week of 48 hours		Proportionate number
During—	Apprentices and improvers	
	s. d.	APPRENTICES
1st year	5 ..	One apprentice to every three or fraction of three workers receiving not less than 25s. per week of 48 hours.
2d "	7 6	
3d "	10 ..	
4th "	12 6	
5th "	15 ..	IMPROVERS
6th "	20 ..	Five improvers to every worker receiving not less than 25s. per week of 48 hours.
	and thereafter the minimum wage	

PIECE-WORK

4. The Board determines under the provisions of Section 144 of the *Factories and Shops Acts* 1912 that any employer may fix and pay piece-work prices to any person or persons or classes of persons employed at any work for which the Board has fixed a minimum wage, provided that any such employer shall base such piece-work prices on the earnings of an average worker working under like conditions, and such piece-work prices shall be fixed so that an average worker can earn not less than the wages that are fixed by the Board for such work.

NOTE.—Cotton and all other materials of which articles provided for in this Determination are made must be supplied by the employer free of charge to the worker, in order that piece-work prices or wages rates payable shall be net.

J. SADLEIR,
Chairman.

Melbourne, October 1, 1913.

INDEX

INDEX

www.ingramcontent.com/pod-product-compliance
Lightning Source LLC
LaVergne TN
LVHW020620110826
845149LV00002B/538

9781418187842